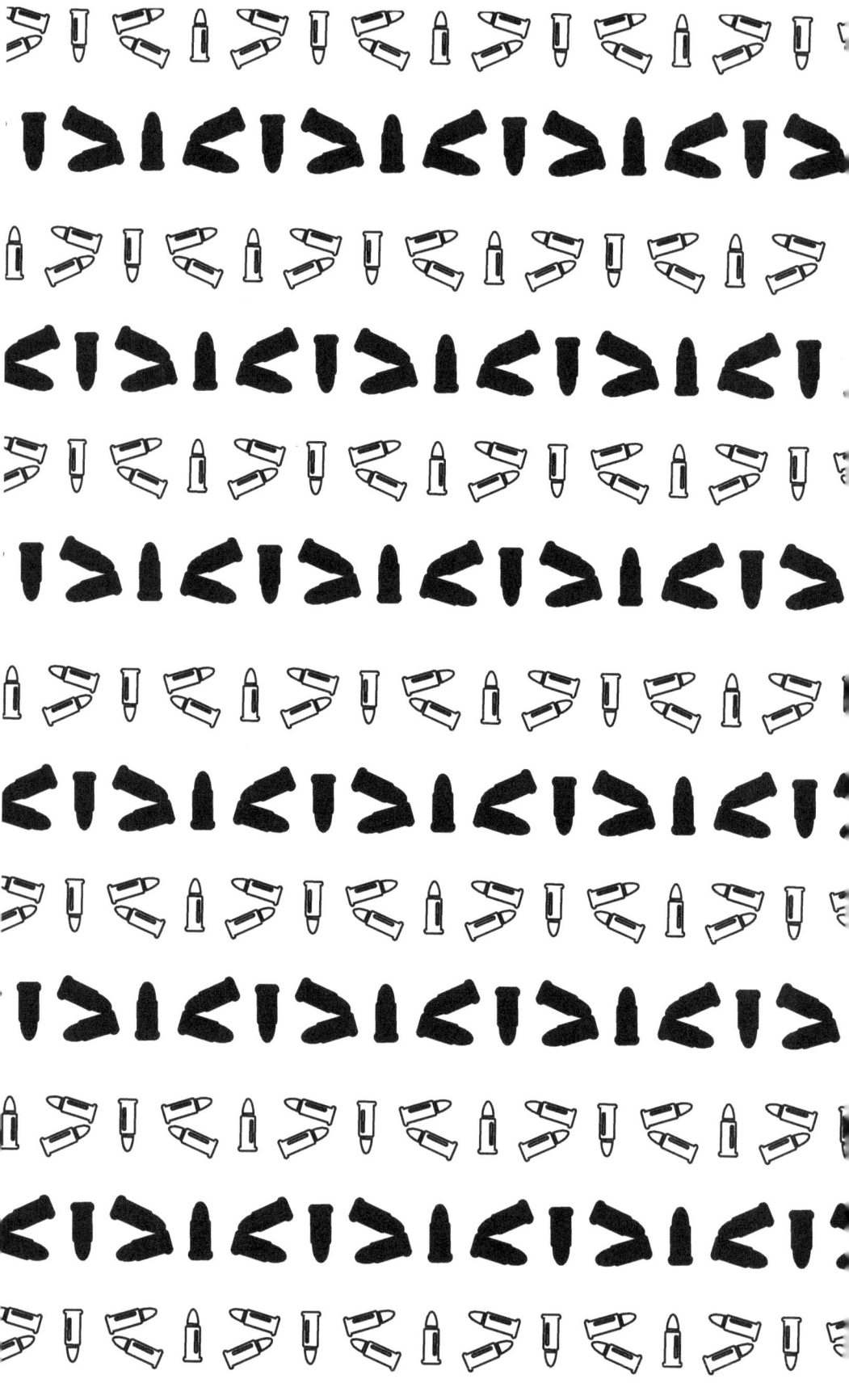

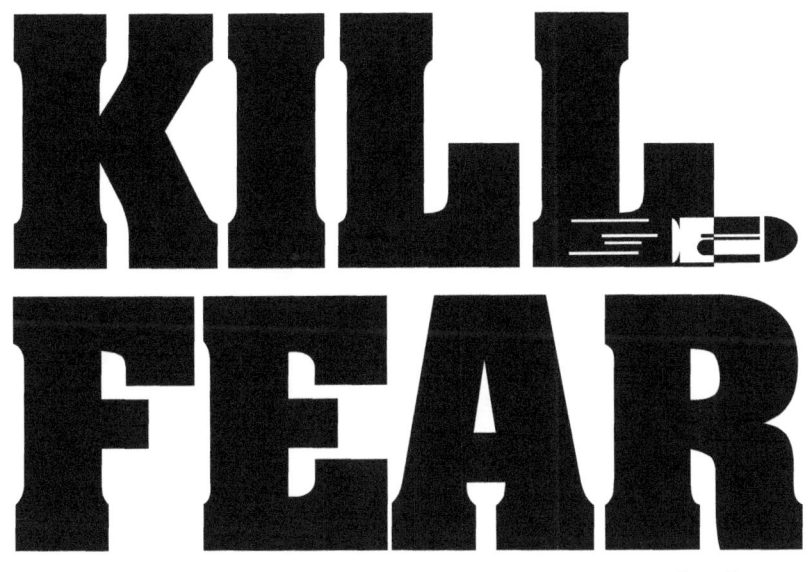

KILL FEAR
The Art of Courageous Living

Krystal Tomlinson

Credits

This is a work of non-fiction. This publication is designed to provide competent and reliable information regarding the subject matter covered. However, it is sold with the understanding that the author and publisher are not engaged in rendering legal, psychological or other professional advice. If legal or expert service is required, a professional should be sought.

Copyright 2018 by Krystal Tomlinson

All Rights Reserved.

Self published in Kingston, Jamaica

Krystaltomlinson.com

Book Cover: Shantay Madden & Grafik Artz
Book Layout: Shantay Madden

Acknowledgements

There is so much gratitude to share in celebration of my first title going to print. The idea to publish a book took root following my participation in the Success Live Conference in late 2017 with my mentee Colleen Chambers. Since then, and with her encouragement, I have gotten to the end of a beautifully empowering process of writing my truth.

As I wrote I reflected on how blessed I am to have encountered so many barriers and failures this early in life. They have proven to be gateways to new heights of success. It may seem counterintuitive but I value every hurdle, challenge and fear. Through each of them I learned to jump, fight and conquer.

To my mother who has been the bravest and fiercest fear-killer I know, thank you. You are my prime example of excellence. You have given me purpose and fuel to live well and fight hard.

To my best friend, Kymberli, you are a bad-ass and I draw so much inspiration from your grit and candid perspective on life and all its lessons. We have travelled a long road together and have seen first hand how our biggest fears and failures have added so much texture and personality to our story.

To Moses, my patient and supportive partner, thank you for believing. Your faith in and love for me frees me from fear every single day.

Table of Contents

PART ONE - **HUNTING: Where is fear?**

- **Chapter 1:** A Declaration of War — page 12
- **Chapter 2:** Friend or Foe? — page 23
- **Chapter 3:** Find the Enemy — page 42

PART TWO - **PHOBICIDE: The killing of fears**

- **Chapter 4:** FOFO — page 60
- **Chapter 5:** FOPO — page 80
- **Chapter 6:** FOMO — page 102

PART

ONE

HUNTING
Where is fear?

CHAPTER ONE
A DECLARATION OF WAR

Fear deserves a vicious and horrible death. It deserves to be burnt alive, in the public square with taunts and ridicule as its final hymn. Fear has terrorised, to no end, some of the most brilliant minds of generations past and present. Fear has developed a reputation of strangling ambition, assassinating self-confidence, poisoning emotional wells and corrupting our view of the world. It is a plague that has developed an almost unrivalled ability to adapt and regenerate, even when we think we have purged the vessel of its stench.

When I say fear deserves a vicious and horrible death, I mean it…***absolutely!***

Can you imagine how different your life would be if you had overcome moments of crippling fear and self-doubt? What if, you had stepped up boldly in public to share your opinion instead of shrinking back because of fear that you might say the wrong thing? Imagine if, instead of doubting your competence, you had shown courage and stepped up for a promotion or vacant post at your office? Your business is probably not where it should be because you are afraid of looking 'unsuccessful' to potential investors, so you won't ask them to invest. Or perhaps, there was excellence at your fingertips but you let it go because you were afraid that you might fail and become the subject of ridicule. Worse yet, you are about to sink another 10 years into a failing relationship because you are afraid of what 'single and starting over' may look like to your friends.

Fear must die hard if we are to live well.

Kill Fear

If we are to fully immerse ourselves in our potential and live a life beyond self and culturally imposed limitations, we must develop a tactical, militant and aggressive approach to cutting down the enemy of our dreams. And that is what this book is about. These ensuing chapters are filled with ammunition and deadly darts aimed at the monster that has been resting inside us for decades. These will become the new marching orders for those of us who refuse to be held hostage by an unseen, ill-equipped, spineless traitor of human potential.

You might think I have gone a bit overboard with the mob-like chant over what can be seen as just an inconvenient emotional stagger, but anyone who has ever gotten to the end of their life, or even the end of the year, and reflected on how well they have lived is always able to recall a moment when they were meant to shine and soar but were made immobile and rendered incontinent by this fear-induced 'stagger'. To those who have let their dreams wash away out of fear of rocking the boat, we know that it is no stagger. It is earth-shattering and soul-crushing and we never wish to share in that moment more than once. Yet, it keeps happening. When we are called upon to lead, to grow, to flourish, we flounder in fear, instead of boldly taking aim and firing from all cylinders into the unknown.

William Shakespeare put it this way:

> *"Our doubts are traitors and make us lose the good we oft might win by fearing to attempt".*

(Shakespeare, 1873, 1.5.Lucio)

Fear has never been associated with any victory worth mentioning or celebrating but it needed to have been conquered internally if any woman or man was to enjoy the freedom of thought, expression and the pursuit of happiness. It is an ever-present predator that lies in wait of our next big idea, our next passion-filled pursuit, ready to pounce, and pillage what little creativity we have left.

If this book does anything for you, my hope is that it equips the warrior within and connects you more divinely with the authority you have to WIN. You deserve victory over your circumstances and strength over your doubts. You have the universe's permission to prosper and live beyond the gory claws of fear. You are meant to feel free, full and fruitful, not what is left after your vessel is raided by the enemy of all things brilliant and bold.

The Rules of Combat

Are you ready to go to war for your dreams; to take up arms for your future and to fight the good fight for the ending you deserve? That feeling you have stirring in your gut, telling you that you must start doing and stop thinking about the success you desire is your potential running wild in your veins. It wants to be unveiled and displayed for the world to see. It is ready to be challenged and put on show. Ready to become a life-giving source, no longer suffocated by the tyranny of fear. Your potential is asking…no, begging you to defend its honour. What will you do now?

You know that the stockpile of reasons is not enough to stop you. You know that if you wanted to change your mind right now, you could!
You know, and that's all that matters. But now that you know, your potential is asking:

"What will you do?"

You might be having trouble coming up with the first step, but that's only because we haven't entered the war chest. There is artillery to help you win this battle, but you need strategy. You can never win the war without developing a strategy that can rebuff the best efforts of a vulture like fear.

1. **Know your enemy.** If you are not aware of fear, its root and routine, it will remain an evasive combatant.
2. **Sharpen your tools.** The enemy is well armed and does not value diplomacy or fair play. You must be ready at all times to attack.
3. **FIRE!** You don't win the war by knowing the plan. You win by executing it. Don't just aim, take a shot.

Once you master this art of war you become a fortress against fear. It doesn't mean fear will never come knocking, but your vessel would have become impenetrable and you will stand, undefeated by the (attempted) assault.

The Warrior's Creed

You are today where your decisions have brought you. The car you drive was a decision. The debts you owe, a decision. Your children, decisions. Your position at the office, decision. None of these things happen without you taking some sort of action. Everything in your current reality, except your DNA and your dependence on oxygen, is present because you chose to do [or not do] something that brought them into your world.

That's a heavy statement and I always get a few rolling eyes and shaking heads when I say it but it doesn't make it any less true. Do I mean you don't get 'lucky breaks' or benefit from the favour of others? Does it mean there is no God and we are all operating on our own accord? No. All those things still happen but if you never take action, even your lucky breaks will stroll right past you.

I have heard adults try to explain how their failures in life are as a result of their parents not being home or leaving them to be raised by a relative or friend. Others insist they are struggling financially because of the Government's bad fiscal policy. I am flush with memories of lively debates that nepotism is the real reason someone missed a promotion so they are stuck in their jobs and unhappy because of…the boss's cousin. They missed the meeting because of traffic or got in late because of the rain. I mean, clearly, no one ever has control over those things. They just happen and make us victims, right?

Wrong.

Let's revisit a few of these examples to see who is really to blame. If you are over 25 years old, and think your failures in life are as a result of your parents, then write down all the decisions that mom or dad still make for you. Are they still choosing your friends? Are they applying for loans in your name and ruining your credit? Are they filling out applications for jobs or degree programmes you don't like? Are they choosing your lovers and marrying you off to people you don't love? Are they handcuffing you to the fridge and telling you not to exercise or dropping unhealthy food in your supermarket trolley that force you to be unwell? If you're one of the four billion people living in a democratic country you may find it difficult to say 'yes' to all of these, but you would need to if you're trying to blame your parents for the current state of your life.

If you are busy blaming anyone for the current state of YOU, you are not ready to save your life!

We are at war and the warrior must take responsibility before she/he can take action.

When your parents fail to give you the attention and guidance you need as a child it presents a disadvantage, but only in childhood. Once you become an adult you not only get permission to vote, drink, drive and seek employment, but you are blessed with an even more powerful tool - CHOICE.

You get to choose if you will work two jobs to pay your way through school or work only one to pay the rent. You get to choose if you will buy liquor to numb the pain of a difficult relationship or save that beer money to start a business.

Either way, the time will pass or the money will be spent. The question is, will time pass and see you two years later with the dreaded beer belly and a damaged liver or with a business, clients and growing income?

Will you still have had a less than desirable childhood? Yes. But you would have also used the power of choice to design a purposeful path forward. You can either allow a lack of love to hinder your growth or water your tree with acts of self-love. You always have that choice. Taking responsibility for your life allows you to access that nourishment.

Nobody threw a lasso around you and dragged you into the life you are living. Instead, every day your actions are dragging you to your destiny.

Your decisions are strongly influenced by what you believe about the world and what you believe about your ability to function in the world. These beliefs are rooted, firmly and absolutely, in your feelings and core philosophy. These roots are fertilised as early as childhood. What you hear, see and experience provide the compost for fertilising feelings and philosophies. And guess what eagerly waters those roots? Love, achievement, loss and **Fear.**

Your philosophies become decisions, then actions, then results. As the results compound, you earn the kind of profit called "life".

So, if you are to kill fear you must stand in a place of ultimate responsibility. You must accept that you are the architect of your future or the one man/woman demolition crew. Just as a soldier goes to war knowing her role on the battlefield, so should you.

You are not just a member of the battalion. You are the commander-in-chief AND a soldier. As in the days of Lionheart, King Richard I of England and many kings, earls, dukes and noblemen before him, the commander is a warrior and not only does he give the charge, as leaders do in this generation, but they lead the charge as the primary defender.

So yes, you will say a prayer and ask your Creator to fill you with the energy, the emotional fortitude, the clarity to see opportunities as they come, and the wisdom to respond appropriately, but you cannot fall asleep when you say 'Amen'. You will prepare to go to war with all the internal forces that prevent you from soaring. You will take the battlefield and defend your mind and heart from that infectious fiend called 'fear'.

If you are ready to take up arms and apply the strategies required then internalise this Warrior's Creed:

I am a warrior. Today and in every tomorrow, I take up arms in defence of my legacy.
I fight for a life less ordinary. For victory over my doubts, insecurities and fear.
The battle ends only in death. Either fear dies or my dreams die.
I will not roll over. I will not sit still.
I will not surrender.
I have what it takes to win this war.
This warrior is ready to do more than aim.
This warrior is ready to FIRE!

Read that again, and let it sink in.

Be prepared for a long and dirty battle. Fear does not fight fairly. You are about to confront the most irrational, unreasonable, elusive yet ubiquitous enemy to ever assault humanity. It plays by its own rules and gives no thought to the casualties that will lie in its wake. This makes it a difficult culprit to tame which is why I do not recommend learning to live peacefully alongside it.

You may have read or heard that a little bit of fear is a good thing. The slight feeling of anxiety when you are about to give a speech that tunes you into the present, and the mood of those around you. That small dose of fear that you feed on just before you enter a new relationship or end a bad one is meant to keep you alert. But if you have never crushed fear, those small doses are sometimes enough to prevent you taking any action. Only the man or woman who has been so bold as to conquer the beast before can perform exceptionally when fear regenerates. Make no mistake; fear will return. It is persistent and confident in its ability to beat you no matter how many times you beat it. What will change upon each visit is not fear, but how you see fear. Your state of mind will either give it strength or cut it down.

If you have never given a successful public presentation, that small serving of fear is enough to make you too ill to leave home. Murdered fear once before? You are confident in your ability to do it again so that 'stage fright' is not so crippling anymore. It is defeated no matter when it shows up because you have become an experienced warrior. The goal is not to get along with fear or exist beside it. The goal is to kill it. Every. Single. Time.

It cannot be trusted with a 'truce' or bribed by reason and logic.

There is no 'getting over it' unless it chooses to stand still, but its unpredictability makes even the attempt to 'get over' too precarious a journey. Kill it, mercilessly.

This approach may be uncommon since growth and development seem to be a naturally non-violent space. It is about life and new beginnings, caterpillars becoming butterflies and barren trees learning to bear fruit. Your success is a series of positive affirmations with almost no talk of killing anything or anyone.

That approach brings many good results but fear, left unchecked, has a way of increasing its intensity and attacking you when you are least prepared. The warrior knows that even when the enemy is at rest, once it exists he is in danger.

You perhaps already know that feeling of thinking you are over or past a particular fear or anxiety and just when you should take things to the next level, fear appears and your ambitions become its spoils.

Fear keeps us comfortable, safe and still. Much like that body of water that has become stagnant, our lives will become a haven for parasites and bacteria and before you know it, we stink. The stench of poor performance, low or no achievement, unfulfilled dreams or failed relationships permeate our very being and we live out our days in resentment and frustration.

If you are to free yourself of its putrid scent, *fear must die - daily.*

This book is your weapon and the eulogy for fear.

CHAPTER TWO
FRIEND OR FOE

But the truth is, we like fear…

If this monster is such a burden to our spirits why have we lived alongside it for this long? Wouldn't we recognise it as an enemy and avoid it at all cost? The answer is yes - but only if we thought fear was an enemy.

For much of human life we have seen fear as a friend because it camouflages itself so well in sheep's clothing. Fear is a very cunning creature, presenting itself as a protector. We have become convinced that fear is there to help us avoid hurt by keeping it real about the risks that lay ahead.

Fear operates on a very mature psychological plane. It has had centuries to perfect its craft and it learns quickly how to manipulate the human mind. But should we pay attention and begin taking copious notes, we could see right through the veil of valiance to the malicious intent it harbours.

Notice how the feeling or thoughts only turn up when you are required to **do** something new or different? If it's just talking, planning and thinking about a new thing, we feel just fine. We are motivated and encouraged to think big and beautiful things. But when it comes time to **do** we get timid at the thought of doing anything that takes us into unfamiliar territory. That is fear at work.

Fear doesn't want you to grow and develop new talents. It doesn't want you taking risks and exiting your comfort zone. Fear has no interest in you becoming your best self. It prefers you just the way you are, exactly where you are. Fear loves you lazy. We learn to do just enough to eke out a living but nothing that is too challenging for our existing routines and habits. We dream of the house we want to live in and speak always of the legacy we will leave for our children and then we get to age 60 and realise we took no meaningful action. We were cemented into mediocrity as we aimed away at our dreams but remained, always, too afraid to fire.

This isn't just an opinion. It is a biological fact. The way our brains are designed, anything that requires complex action or relearning intimidates our cognitive circuitry. The brain is a very advanced tool that is constantly seeking efficiency. It has a special cupboard where it stores habits, patterns and memories called the basal ganglia. There is also a separate compartment that is activated when new things are to be learned - the prefrontal cortex. This prefrontal lobe is responsible for decision making, planning and measuring our behaviour for social appropriateness. To increase efficiency, the brain shuts down the prefrontal lobe once a behaviour or pattern has been learned and stores it in that basal ganglia cupboard.

So if you have a new habit to form or an old habit to kill, the prefrontal cortex is the raw flame that purges, refines and cooks this new behaviour into your psyche. Your basal ganglia is the microwave that quickly reheats the new knowledge when needed. As an efficiency seeking organ, you can understand why the brain would prefer the quick reheat as opposed to using energy to cook a brand new meal. That sensation of fear is wrapped into the natural resistance your brain has to doing things differently. Fear feeds on that resistance to change and is depending on you to leave things as they are. To kill fear you have to fight your predisposition to remain in your comfort zone.

The fearful saviour

One of the great tragedies of human potential is that we spend hours planning and working for the success of everyone around us and not for our own dreams. We mechanically show up in the service of others - children, parents, siblings, employers - well dressed, well trained and ready to work for their growth and excellence and feel like noble martyrs as we put our ambitions aside to better the community. We honestly believe that by doing all for everyone we are somehow doing the best thing for our spirit. Charity and kindness are their own virtue but there is no virtue or glory to be had in playing small and hiding our light.

When we get friendly with the enemy, it cajoles us into thinking that by standing in the back and keeping our mouths shuts and our ideas hidden we are helping others to do better. Have you ever convinced yourself that you needed to continue doing something because if you stopped someone else would suffer? Instead of continuing because you enjoy it or it helps you to grow, you're doing it because you don't want someone else to suffer.

That's not chivalry. That's fear. Fear of what doing the right thing means. Fear that living true to your conscience might upset the apple cart. So, friendly, fear says, "In the best interest of your friendship, marriage, job, or family, let's not do this" - and you listen. It keeps you from having awkward conversations and from taking difficult decisions. Fear keeps you comfortable.

What's the harm in that? Why upset the apple cart if things are fine as they are? Because no one wants to remain in the same place, with the same people, doing the same things all their life.

We want growth. We are stimulated by change. We are sharpened by challenges and fear is the kind of corrupt compass that leads you far away from any of those growth stimulants. Whatever puts pressure on that muscle of progress comes with discomfort and so it is easy to associate the magnetic pull of growth with anxiety and stress. It is unknown territory and a place of vulnerability, so fear counsels you to remain exactly where you are, amidst what you know, and that can feel friendly.

No good friend tells you to avoid going to school because learning is difficult and you might fail at it. No good friend tells you to stay in an unhealthy relationship because being single looks bad to other people. No good friend tells you to give up on your dream because you don't have what it takes to be successful. The kind of person who does that is the kind who wants to see you settle for less than you are capable of having.

Fear is strongest and most resilient when we are attempting to exit our comfort zone; when we are looking to do something grand and meaningful. Fear can be very resilient when it is aiming at your ambitions. It seems almost impenetrable when you try to break it apart. When you are attempting a small and inconsequential thing, fear is quickly demolished, but seek to achieve a big, bold goal and fear seems as imposing as the goal itself. It expands and reinforces itself just as you are seeking to expand and excel.

So what do we often do **when fear gets big?** We retreat and surrender:

- **Aim at smaller targets (retreat)**
- **Settle for less than we are capable of (retreat)**
- **Convince ourselves that we aren't ready (retreat)**
- **Walk away from our passions and pursue primary goals (surrender)**

And here's the bonus move…

- **Negotiate others out of their big dreams**

We become such experts at why and how to retreat and surrender that it becomes our gospel, preached fervently into the hearts of those who we can convince to back down and call it quits. One definition of fear is:

> *An unpleasant emotion caused by the threat of danger, pain or harm.*

Your body is feeling as though you are about to enter the danger zone; as though a rabid hyena is chasing you through the desert - because you are ready to commit to a new relationship, change your diet, or start a business. Fear is telling you that your life is at risk for taking a chance on your dreams.

How unreasonable is that?! It's silly really, but it doesn't mean we don't believe the absurdity. Knowing that it's silly doesn't make us any more buoyant and eager to run wildly into the unknown glory of a worthy goal being pursued and achieved. And in the moment we allow that increased heart rate, sweaty palms, heightened blood pressure and tightened muscles to cripple us, we give fear power. If we refuse to confront the deceiver it will devour our zest for life and leave us with two options:

- Wrestling to regain control, snatching our dreams from fear's filthy claws **or**
- Admitting defeat and walking away from that which we desire the most.

It is an uphill battle, and steeper yet, depending on how well-fed fear has been over the years; how beefy and plump and strong fear has gotten from consuming and destroying our ambitions and opportunities for joy and love. But the steep hill and muddy battlefield is not too much for you to handle if you are well prepared. So, let's get armed for war.

Part of our perpetual failure in handling this monster is that we are firing aimlessly. We need more precision. Your first task is to get clear and honest with yourself. It's not cute anymore, this dragging of your feet and living below your potential. It embarrasses everyone who has ever made an investment in you and adds no glory to the effort of the Creator who opened the world up to you through your precious life. You are worthy of victory. You have no reason to sit back and take it…or watch fear take it from you. In this moment you need to get bold and stare fear squarely in the eyes. Get familiar with what it looks and feels like and why it has this much power over your life.

This will be difficult but remember, this is your life and if you won't go to war for it, who will? No one can fight this for you. Even with support, direction, prayer and spiritual fortitude, you will lose this battle if you never take a step towards the enemy. Fear is expecting you to back down and surrender but the warrior in you still has some fight left. Get a pen and let's get clear. It's time to identify and demolish the cause of our suffering.

The cost of my fear

My biggest fear is _____

_____

_____

_____

_____

_____.

This fear of _____

_____

_____

_____

_____

has robbed me of _____

_____

and _____

_____

_____.

I allowed fear to overpower me and now I am _____

_____

_____.

Now that you've named and shamed it, how do you feel? Take some time to reflect on that emotion. Is it relief, guilt, embarrassment, surprise? Confront the emotion and then project yourself into the future. When you kill that fear, how will you feel afterwards?

When fear dies I will feel _____

_____

_____!

And you're absolutely right! This will not be a battle fought and forgotten. You will relish the results for years to come.

Kill Fear

I learned this lesson at age 20, my third year in University and my first time as a lone competitor on the international stage.

I have always been a vibrant and outspoken young woman, just like everyone else.

Before you tell me you are shy and introverted, let me explain why I say "everyone" else. We are all leaders in our comfort zone. We are experts, teachers, trainers and counsellors in the areas of our lives that bring us the least challenge. So if you are extremely shy in class, you may be very outspoken in your dance or theatre group where you feel comfortable. If you hardly speak to your coworkers, you are likely to be very chatty with your siblings at the family dinner in December. If you run from the spotlight at social events, you're perhaps the loudest voice at the Friday night karaoke where you know for sure that you can belt out the worst possible notes and still be applauded.

We all have evidence of being vibrant and outspoken, loud and obnoxious; jolly and extroverted. Those examples often emerge when we enter a space of comfort, control and low/no judgement. We play small and aim low when we are in unfamiliar territory. We play small to turn down the sound of failure in case anyone should see us attempt a new and difficult thing. So I'm vibrant and outspoken- like everyone else!

At age 20 when I was called to play big, I was nervous and afraid of failing because there would be many people on hand to see me attempt a great thing and (possibly) fail. It was 2010 and this little Jamaican was in Botswana to compete in the World Public Speaking Competition as part of a global debate championships for universities across the world.

My campus - The University of the West Indies, Mona - had never taken home the title and this was my first time entering. I had attended the event the year before and done all I could to avoid entering a competition whose title was often copped by the Princeton, Oxford and Yale entrants. And so, the ants in my cupboard went to work.

Fear haunted me in 2009 by reminding me that I wasn't good enough…yet. I needed more experience, more time, more training, if I should even hope to make it to the finals. Fear told me that I was from the Caribbean so no one would understand my accent. Fear told me I was a black female and this was a white male's domain. Fear told me my school was barely on the map and my competitors were the brightest of the best universities in the world. Fear told me I wasn't well read enough to make an extemporaneous presentation in the five-minute window each participant received. Fear told me no one I knew had ever done it, and there was nothing special about me that could change the course of history.

Fear made a convincing argument and I was deliberately unavailable for the first round of the competition that year. In a moment that called on me to let loose my talents and allow my voice to be heard and even be celebrated, I became a prisoner of war.

The Self-Imposed Prison

While the circumstances I described above are not common to everyone, the internal conversations certainly are. That habit of being our biggest critic and the most vocal opponent of doing something new and different is one we have all mastered to the point of perfection. We do not need someone else to discourage us. In fact, we make it our duty to do it first; before anyone else has the honour of making us feel significant. We are purposely racing to cross that finish line of self-defeating self talk before anyone else does.

Unfortunately, when we fail to encourage our excellence the world accommodates us.

The Temptation to Underperform

The first two decades of the 21st Century will come to be defined as a "Grand Global Performance". The popularity and reach of social media platforms have provided a stage for new character development and the re-scripting of lives to satisfy the ever-growing audience. We "share" our way to great fanfare and calls for an encore as the world double-taps its way to affirming, celebrating and rewarding the best performers among us. And all that comes at no real cost to the performer. The primary tools of stagecraft have become good lighting, superb angles and data to share the production. Very little effort, work, result or excellence is needed to feel as though we have done something spectacular.

What we find is a growing display of grand mediocrity at the expense of excellence. What we post as #Goals and #RoleModels differ from the aspirations of our parents who thought more critically of the legacy to be enjoyed by their families. From parents who did it "for the fam" to those who now do it "for the gram", the gap widens between the ethos of the generation before ours and the one we are grooming to lead. The drive to **create** something excellent has been replaced by the desire to **show** that we have taken part in or consumed something excellent.

We observe when we should initiate and consume when we should create and still get the applause and envy that was once reserved for those with the creative consciousness to produce. That is not a recipe for excellence but rather a popularly sung medley of mediocrity. Only a few refuse to be impressed by the show and they are called "conscious" and "woke". I call them the **authentic minority**.

The Authentic Minority is unbothered by the criticism that will come when people see them building, struggling and earning their excellence. They are unmoved by the **allodoxaphobia** that keeps others stationed at the post of mediocre life goals and meaningless wins. The Authentic Minority sees failure as the temporary discomfort that exists only on the "Achievement Avenue". For that select few, no failure means no growth and so the fear of failure would equate to the fear of improvement. Their view of the enemy makes them stronger than the threat at hand. So instead of fearing failure, fear being complicit in this crime against progress called conformity.

It hardly matters what is "expected" in a world where mediocrity is celebrated and excellence is viciously scrutinized. You'll want to fit in, to be regular and normal and liked and all the boring things that under-performers are always talking about. #BLAH! Tell them you're not interested and refuse to be impressed by anything less than excellence. Then you'll start living like you mean it!

Kill Fear

The Authentic Minority routinely kills fear.

So where do you fall? Among the Authentic Minority or the Mediocre Majority? Among the killers of fear or those killed by it?

Based on your position on the battlefield - armed to act or retreating in fear of defeat - you earn immediate membership in one of these battalions.

Your power will not come through peaceful surrender to your feeling of discomfort and uncertainty. Whenever you feel fear seasoning and marinating your potential, readying to enjoy another meal at the expense of your dreams, know with certainty that it is a call to the battlefield and like any soldier fighting to defend a prized territory you must show up to protect what is yours.

If your dreams matter, fight fear and protect them! Your excuses shouldn't mean more than your opportunity for excellence. You impose upon your ambitions a sense of detention and imprisonment that will delay or completely defeat your opportunity for growth. In the moment you choose not to brandish a weapon and become an active combatant, you are volunteering for your tomorrows to become POWs - Prisoners of War.

Learn to spot the enemy as it approaches, learn to aim strategically at its core and be brave enough to fire shots when it matters most.

Shots fired...enemy down!

Back to Botswana, with me trying to escape the self-imposed prison. I fired some shots at fear and took on the challenge to be seen.

I entered the competition and moved past round 1 with ease. Round two was just as easily conquered and before the night of the finals, the word on the ground was that I would win. The only matter was whether my Jamaican teammate would place second - an even sweeter victory to return home with a double whopper.

As I sat there among all the well-read finalists waiting to hear the topic and prepare my 3-minute speech, would you believe that fear paid me a visit? I was in the winner's circle and fear had the audacity to come and sit with me. I don't know that it visited anyone else but it came for me with guns blazing. Fear congratulated me on my 'luck' getting into the finals! I was being told that I had not made it there because of my own excellence and hard work but because I was 'lucky'. Maybe a judge was simply enamoured with my afro hairstyle. Maybe the Jamaican girl was exotic to them, and they just wanted to hear that island accent one more time. Maybe it's because you are a female and they didn't want it to be a bull-fest so you're just the "token" woman. Whatever the reason, luck was on my side but this was as far as it would take me.

My palms began to sweat even more than usual and my make-up became very clammy under my neck. By now, I was looking around to see if my competitors looked uncomfortable too and sure enough, they all seemed quite fine. But why wouldn't they be? They had earned their spot. I had just lucked out! And so my next move was to see if I could pick the winner so I wouldn't be surprised when they were announced victorious. At least that wouldn't catch me off guard. I accepted the surety of failure even before I made my presentation. I don't know that I actively listened to anyone who spoke before or after me because either way, they were making a winning speech. I was just trying to remember the correct subject/verb agreement and avoid saying "uuhhm" as I mentally constructed a decent opening sentence. My goal was simple - don't get laughed at. I would lose with dignity. The story would not be told along the lines of "…you remember when that Jamaican girl said…OMG! I nearly died!"

So I spoke. I spoke well. There was applause but I was cautious. Fear was sitting with me, in the end, to assure me that they were only being polite. They clapped for everyone. In the end, I won; the first female in the Caribbean and Latin America to cop the title. When I received the award, I was still shocked. In the months following, I was not yet a believer in me because I still couldn't tell you how I won. There was a part of me that still thought I had gotten lucky while everyone and their sister kept telling me they knew I would do it.

And that's when my debate coach made a very powerful statement. One I remember every time I plan to water down my excellence and skill. He said, "Krystal, your playing small does not serve the world." He had a very sobering look on his face that went on to tell me it was an injustice to pretend that I was not worthy. I was doing something wrong that embarrassed those who believe in me and the One who created me. I did not feel empowered by the statement. I felt ashamed that I was cowering while the world celebrated a good thing I had done. In that moment I vowed to never shrink back for fear of losing. I would not limit my potential because fear spoke loudly in my ear. I would use the evidence of my success to launch me into a new atmosphere of earned excellence and deserved distinction. I stopped looking for the evidence of weakness in my character and focused on my strengths. I reminded myself of the times I did well and refused to ruminate on the things I did not-so-well. ***I killed fear by changing my mind about myself.***

I took on the power of self-definition and re-created my character, habits and beliefs to match the 'me' I wanted to be.

One powerful fact that drives home the unique place that we are meant to hold in this world is the calculation of the odds of our existence. Scientists estimate that we went up against the odds of one in 400 trillion. The more I researched this probability I realised how narrowly I missed coming into this world. Of all the people in the world, my mother and father met each other. In a split second, they could've missed each other - or one could have decided not to leave the house that day - and not met at all and that would mean I wouldn't exist.

Of the partners each of them had met and dated they chose to have children together. But the odds get even worse! What if a different sperm had penetrated the egg? I would certainly not be me. The DNA, talent, physical attributes, mental capacity, and emotional states would have made for a completely different human. The odds that I am made this way are absolutely frightening - one in 400 quadrillions. (Binzair, 2011)

The motto of the King's Guard in Ancient Greece: "All men have fear, but the brave put down their fears and go forward, sometimes to death, but always to victory." I died a little by putting down my fears but those parts deserved to die anyway.

Refuse to live within the limits of your fears. Deny fear the opportunity to set your standards and determine your destiny. Rely not on the evidence of your fallibility, but on the proof of your power to conquer.

> *I refuse to live within the limits of my fears. I deny fear the opportunity to set my standards and determine my destiny. I will not rely on the evidence of my fallibility but on the proof of my power to conquer. I will kill fear!"*

My Secret Sauce

Self-definition has proven to be a resilient mental machine-gun when I get fearful of what lies on the other side of a big decision. I honestly believe that I am a 3D Powerhouse. I define myself as daring, dynamic and deliberate and I have it set as a reminder in my phone that goes off at 9am every morning. My daily alarm to get working on my projects used to say "Work" but now it says "Daring, Dynamic and Deliberate" and it reminds me of the layers of my personality that I want to define me; how I wish to be remembered. It reminds me of the eulogy I want to earn when my life comes to an end.

When fear tries to create a wedge between me and a new opportunity, I call on the reminder that I am daring. It becomes a declaration that I am willing to do uncommon, uncomfortable and unfamiliar things even if I don't have all the knowledge and experience that would make me more confident. It is pointed directly at any fear that lies in wait of a big dream so whenever I feel the urge to delay because of discomfort or fear, I say out loud, "Remember, you're daring". That encourages my boldness, temerity and audacity.

Define yourself powerfully and use words and phrases that have nothing to do with your job, spouse, children or education. That definition must inspire you if it is to get closer to you than your fears. Always be ready to attack those feelings of "not good enough" with a reminder of who you are or who you plan to become. Be pushed into action by the clarity of knowing thyself.

Always be ready to attack those feelings of "not good enough" with a reminder of who you are or who you plan to become. Be pulled into action by the clarity of knowing thyself.

CHAPTER THREE
FIND THE ENEMY

-Where are these ants coming from?

Any good housekeeper will tell you that one of the most baffling things to uncover after months or years of good housekeeping is how the ants got in. You can wipe down every surface and sweep away all stray grains of sugar but somehow, someday, there is an organised troop of ants marching to and from the pantry. It is no fault of hers as she has kept no dirty cupboard, countertops or floors. Her diligence is unquestionable so it must mean one thing, right? Ants are magically appearing!

Well, perhaps it's not magic. Perhaps it's something a little less conspicuous, yet far more profound than that. When the exterminator comes to smoke them out, notice they don't look in the pantry. Have you ever wondered why they begin everywhere else but where you tell them to look? Their professional experience tells them that the final destination is hardly ever the source if your house is well kept.

If your house is unkempt with signs of neglect and poor housekeeping it is less of a mystery. The homeowner knows deep down that calling an exterminator will only highlight their own failings and so instead of reaching for help they would rather clean up a little bit first to see if the environment is inviting the insects to dinner a la carte.

But for the responsible homeowner, the pieces of the puzzle don't fit so well. The exterminator will soon explain that ants make their way into our pantries through four main gateways:

- Gaps in the Foundation
- Cracks in the Wall

Kill Fear

- Toys brought in from the playground
- They were born in the house

Now the housekeeper hardly thinks to check these four gateways and so will often miss that first sign of ants moving in.

Consider yourself the housekeeper; the house, your very being; the pantry your mind; the ants, your fears and the four gateways the entrance through which you allow fear to enter and fester within those walls. The exterminator will be anyone we call for help, depending on how badly infected we are with fear. But that person whom you wish to help you will be rendered ineffective because, unlike an exterminator, you can walk through every corner and nook in your home to spot the fault. No one, not even the pastor who is divinely inspired, can see through you to make that assessment.

This leaves only one person who can truly take action to remove the pests about to invade - you. Only you can walk the very corners of your mind and interrogate your walls, foundation, doors, floors and all things beneath and before. You are the person best equipped to manoeuvre the maze and find the flaws. The only question is, will you do it or will fear of the effort and commitment cripple you into inaction and hand over control of your life and energy to this "thing"?

If you won't do it then who will? Your Creator gave you this beautiful mind filled with power and potential and He expects you to make the best use of it. So, will you fail to honour even that omniscient confidence vested in you?

It is time to arm yourself with the tools and attitudes of a life on purpose. Identify the source of your fears, cut the enemy off at its feet and spend more of your life running towards your victories and maybe even a few defeats - on your terms.

Remember the guidance given in 1 Timothy 1:7 - "For God has not given us a spirit of fear, but of power, love and a sound mind."

Your Creator gave you this beautiful mind filled with power and potential and He expects you to make the best use of it. So will you fail to honour even that omniscient confidence vested in you?

Gaps in the foundation

We are all built on something. Each of us walking this earth stands on a foundation, weak or strong, that determines how we will build our lives. Before we become conscious of our thoughts; we begin to create a foundation that will last us a lifetime without recognising it. There is such beauty in a mind that can assimilate, interpret and store information without being told to do so. That is the power of the machine we so thoughtlessly take for granted each day. The way your mother spoke to you. The way your father treated your mother. The way dinner was shared and the proportions given to each at the table. The way friends embraced your ideas or bullies rejected your quirkiness. The way teachers listened or strangers shut you up. A myriad of experiences rest in our psyche and shine the light on who we will become. With our foundation out of our control, as most things are for the young and impressionable, we look back on our formative years and remember only hallmark moments of deep emotional pain or pleasure. Many times we reflect in extremes remembering the happiest times, scariest moments, most embarrassing reprimands and wildest celebrations.

These are equally as valuable as the mundane routines and patterns of those around us. The ones we thought we ignored but they somehow crept into our subconscious and left indelible marks on our perception of ourselves and the world.

Aristotle, over 2,400 years ago, contemplated that to know one's self is the beginning of all wisdom and a core component of who we are is based on who influenced us in those years of youth and ignorance.

Take a moment to reflect on how your teachers responded to you when you had ideas as a child. Did they make light of them, calling them frivolous or childish? Or did they encourage you by engaging in discussions that stimulated that idea? The answers to those questions weigh heavily on why you fear speaking up in a meeting. You may have gotten used to your ideas being dismissed and belittled. Fear has crept in through your foundation.

Did you grow up in a household where one parent bent over backwards to please and serve the other and was content to sacrifice what they wanted so the other could thrive or at least be more comfortable? If so, you may find yourself over-extending in your friendships and intimate relationships as you mimic that early example of 'love', fearing that any other approach might find you living out your days alone. That inevitably opens you up to abuse and manipulation. Fear has crept in through your foundation.

If during your teenage years you were painfully betrayed by a friend you trusted dearly, you can understand why you have such anxiety and fearfulness when entering new relationships - intimate or platonic. Fear has crept in through your foundation.

The psychology of self-identity reveals that we are shaped by our experiences. We are clay and they give shape to our tone, texture and lens as we travel life's scenic and treacherous road. Without a solid start, we stagger in our lane, not understanding why 'getting it right' seems an impossible feat. Your foundation is your start, but thankfully it does not have to be your end. No matter what truth you are coming from, there is a better truth that awaits. The power of choice, the most defining element of our existence, affords us a new compass to change our trajectory entirely.

You are not stuck with your past as a pathway. You can change course at any moment. You are not too old to choose excellence. You are not too young to cut a new stairway to success. You are not unprepared for the work of a winner. Right now, where you are, who you are and what you have are all you need to create a life worth living if you make your choices from a place of courage instead of a place of fear.

Cracks in the wall

We are prone to missing the little things. The sound of new birds as the seasons change; the smell of morning on a bright summer day; the smooth waft of wind that ruffles the curtains. We miss it all because we are looking at the big things. How many of us realise those big things are made of small things compounded over time?

Like the wind we ignore, coming through the window, which returns at gale force in a hurricane, so too do small blows to our psyche compound over time taking on a profound intensity. But we recognise it only when it becomes too big to ignore. That drip-drip-drop in the kitchen sink from a leaky faucet that soon becomes the source of rotting wood and damaged floors is simply a little thing that has grown to become a big thing. And it is not that we never see the little thing as it happens. It is just that our brains have not registered it as worthy of note, so we effortlessly glide by without realising the drips coming at shorter intervals. Our minds will ignore stimulus that it is unable to use in the moment for decision-making. Unless we take the time to notice when little faults develop in our beautiful frame, there is no saving the pantry from those nefarious ants.

So what are those little things? It's the self-deprecating conversation we have with ourselves that makes us feel unworthy because we made an error in judgement. It's the painful chiding from someone we love who never speaks of our good but bitterly laments the bad. It's the friend who doesn't stand with us in our time of need. It's the way a stranger judges us without giving us an opportunity to even speak. It's the employer that slams a door in our face when we feel economically vulnerable. It's the unsolicited comment under an Instagram photo that points out a flaw you had long forgotten. The crack in the wall gets deeper and wider the more we pretend that it doesn't hurt, and the more we act as though we didn't see or hear that pretence and false confidence only put a veil over the emotional wound, and we look around one day to find that we have become deathly afraid of the judgement of others.

This is evidence of an unconscious conditioning that trains us to conform. After repeated exposure to negative stimuli we will eventually recoil into ourselves in anticipation of the consequence of our action. We get so used to being shut down or shut up that we never bother to stand up or speak out because we are now sure of how it will end.

In that moment, we decide not to act because those feelings of ridicule, neglect and criticism rob us of what little confidence we have left. That is proof that fear has arrived. There is no painting over the cracks in the wall. Once it exists and is left un-repaired it is like a picnic table for an army of ants to make their way into your emotional pantry and corrupt every good thing in sight.

Toys from the playground

I have never met someone who didn't like a gift; if even the gift of a listening ear, time, a good word or a smile. Gifts come in small and large packages but once they strike the right emotional chord, no matter the size, we will make space for it.

A child at play, in her most joyous mood, will share her jubilation with her playmate by giving away her toys. It is her gift to a new found friend or comrade. Yet, I remember getting a slap on the hand for returning home with toys I didn't leave home with or even with none of mine at all!

I could not understand what ignoble thing I had done by simply accepting a gift or trading gifts with my friends. Wasn't that what friends did?

My mother's response would often be "Leave people with their things. You have your own. Learn to be satisfied." But no child understands the word satisfied, do they? It is almost as though there were an infinite vortex to be filled that no amount of toys or trinkets could appease. This word satisfaction made no sense. There is always space for one more nice thing.

So too do we make excuses to invite new people into our lives to fill whatever vacant slot we have. These new people, or toys, however you wish to describe them, carry with them energies that soon stain our own aura, both positively and negatively. Just as ants come in on toys from the playground, so too will fear travel on the backs of others who become our trusted confidantes and friends. It soon becomes difficult to separate your emotional condition from theirs and as simple as it is for you to share your passion for sewing, so will they effortlessly introduce you to their own toxicity.

On the playground they were vibrant, energetic and buoyant, but as time passes you begin to feel drained by their very presence and unsuspectingly adopt their way of thinking, being and doing. Keep your guard up. As exciting as it is to add one more friend to your circle, be wary of the energy you bring into your intimate surroundings. They often bring more than you went in the market for. Curate with doggish deliberation the friendships you maintain. With almost military-type precision, test rigorously the premise of each new friendship. If you find there is more harm than good that comes with anyone then take my mother's advice and leave people with their things. You have your own! We all have our own insecurities, doubts and fears assaulting us with regularity. Learn to be satisfied with your burden and not seek to take home more than you can bear.

It is also necessary to assess who we are attracting and what about our own energy makes unhealthy characters comfortable around us. What signals are you sending in your environment that communicate that you are willing to entertain certain conversations, relationships and treatment? Before you ask "why me" when you are disappointed by these relationships answer the more powerful question - "What was it about me?"

As you decide who will stay, choose people who water your roots with rich spiritual nutrients with no intention of sharing in the harvest. These are the kinds of friends who inspire you to act and live out your ambitions. They are offended when you are mediocre and disappointed - when you live timidly. Your fear is the most unattractive thing to them because they would rather see you fearless. Your success is their success just because they are close enough to see you enjoy richly the blessings you deserve.

They were born in the house

I want you to read this story and tell me what you think. Stephen is a bright young man who has always enjoyed the respect and admiration of his peers. He was never exceptional at any particular thing but people liked him. His family was supportive, his friends loyal and his co-workers respectful. He has never been told that he doesn't have what it takes to succeed and so he developed within himself a burning desire to always do his best, on projects great or small.

Despite Stephen's amicable personality and good work ethic, he is laid off during a redundancy exercise at his job, along with many other bright men and women. The Human Resource Manager goes to great lengths to assure Stephen that he had been a very competent employee however the company simply could not afford to keep him on as their profits were well below target for nearly ten years.

Kill Fear

Stephen spends 8 weeks looking for opportunities and keeps his outlook positive. He applies for several vacancies in his field and secures a few interviews, but still no callbacks. On one particular morning, he walks into a firm that he considers the premier business place to work because of the benefits they offer employees and the fact that they have a strong culture of promoting their internal staff once they have shown potential for growth. He is most excited about this interview because this is the ideal job, in the ideal place. Two days after the interview he receives a call to say that he was not selected for the position but that he was one of the stronger contenders.

He calls his friend to share how disappointed he was and to his surprise, his friend responded, "Well what did you expect? Why did you think you were good enough to even work there? You barely had any success in your last job and no one wants to hire someone who has been fired. It's proof that you weren't an asset to the last company. Why would they think you could be an asset to them?"

He continued, "Steve, you know the calibre of people at that office. They are outstanding and exceptionally qualified and you don't fit that description. Set your sights lower, man. Stop setting yourself up for embarrassment with all this ambition. Stay in your lane and play in your league. Maybe you should apply for entry-level positions moving forward. It's been over 2 months. It's time to get real."

So, Stephen gives it up. He aims small and stays at the bottom, avoiding every opportunity to stand out because that was out of his league. His good friend told him so.

What would you do if that was your friend?

_____

_____

_____

_____

_____.

Now, what if I told you that Stephen had that conversation with himself? He called no friend about it. He just sat down and said those things to himself. He chose to pour gas on his own self-esteem, light it and let it burn. He convinced himself that he had nothing to offer and shrunk back into the darkness of self-imposed defeat. How many times have we done that to ourselves?

What things have you been telling yourself about you? And why did you believe yourself? Don't get comfortable with your opinion of yourself. We are dead wrong more than half the time about most things in life. That also applies to what we think we can achieve. We spend too much time reeling from defeat instead of standing on the lessons. Because we pore over the mistakes and pour gas on our spirit, we miss the magic of wisdom unfolding even in our worst moments.

Because we have lived with ourselves for decades we assume that we know all there is to know about our capabilities and our potential.

Kill Fear

How many times have we told ourselves that it's over when it's just beginning, simply because we are afraid to make ourselves vulnerable to the criticism and rejection of strangers. Can you imagine the irony? Because we are afraid of being criticised, we suffocate our talents and ambitions.

Know this, as an absolute fact. There is no opinion so powerful as the one you have of yourself. So be very careful of who you think you are.

The words of King Solomon in Proverbs 31 are often paraphrased to say "As a man thinketh, so is he."

Alfred Lunt from the script of Reunion in Vienna said: "there is nothing I need more such as nourishment for my self-esteem." These excerpts present sage advice. We must feel like winners if we are to win. Triumph is first had on the battlefields of the mind.

There is no shortage of truths to be quoted on the matter of protecting yourself from your thoughts, but this final quote hits home for me every time:

"Without confidence, man is twice defeated in the race of life" ~Marcus Mosiah Garvey, Black Nationalist and Jamaican National Hero.

You see, it is this final circumstance that amplifies the potential for destruction. Having crept in through the foundation, cracks and toys, your nurturing it allows new tentacles to take root and that is a dangerous ecosystem.

As the walls become infested and the foundation shows its flaws and the people around us weigh us down, we must have the kind of mental fortitude that provides no nutrients for this pestilence called fear. For if we do, we create the ultimate five-star environment for fear to flourish and cut us off from our power to prosper.

END OF CHAPTER ACTIVITY

How has fear entered your life? What parts of your mental 'home' need urgent attention to save yourself from internal defeat and under-performance?

This exercise is emotionally and mentally taxing, requiring deep introspection of scars and trauma that may not have been recognised, tended or healed. Take some time to reflect honestly and complete the table below.

Source of fear	The Fear	3 things fear prevents me from doing/causes me to do		
Foundation	I was raised in a household where we had just enough to make it through the month. I thought that I would never have enough money to meet my needs because wealth was far removed from my family	I spent wantonly having accepted that I would never have enough	I made no attempt to save because it seemed pointless	I incurred debt at every opportunity as though it were my only option to sustain myself

Kill Fear

Source of fear	The Fear	3 things fear prevents me from doing/causes me to do		
Foundation				
Cracks	As a child, my brother teased me about having corns on my toes and for about 18 years I never wore sandals. I was afraid others would see and embarrass me.	I refused to wear sandals	I hid my feet from my partner because I anticipated being judged and ridiculed as unattractive	I envied those who I thought had more beautiful feet than I did
Toys from the playground				

The Art of Courageous Living

Source of fear	The Fear	3 things fear prevents me from doing/causes me to do
Born in the house		

I've filled out a sample column to guide you through this exercise. As we move through subsequent chapters you will be able to identify and sharpen your tools so you can live life on your terms, faith-filled and fear-free.

PART

TWO

PHOBICIDE
The killing of fears

CHAPTER FOUR
FAILURE

I want the money, the cars and the clothes…I suppose I just wanna be successful. Those words were put to a beautiful melody by Trey Songz and Drake in 2009. When we talk about our desire for success we expose to the world the things we fear living without. That list of ambitions and aspirations, while telling the tale of what success means to us, will inevitably reveal what failure means as well.

F.O.F.O. - Fear of Flunking Out

You've heard the references. Michael Jordan being cut from his basketball team in high school but going on to become the greatest player of the game. Steve Jobs being fired from his own company but returning as a maverick in the tech industry. JK Rowling being turned down by publisher after publisher before her Harry Potter series made her a billionaire.

Somehow these references don't seem to mean much when we encounter our own personal failures. Telling ourselves that the wealthy fail too is just not enough to give us wings. There is something special about them that makes their experience different. They were white, they were males, they were American, so they have cultural advantages that give them access to privilege. It is difficult for us to accept that there could be any real relationship between our existence and theirs.

They might be the ideal comeback kids but you're just not built that way.

What a different world it would be if Martin Luther King Jr. thought that way. Imagine if he was too afraid of all the things working against him to challenge unjust laws in America. What a different world, indeed. Such a mammoth task and with so much evidence to prove that failure was all but guaranteed, yet he persisted. Can you imagine a world still lit by candles and kerosene lamps? That may well have been a constant reality had Thomas Edison not been such a lover of failure, insisting that he could create a commercially viable light bulb. So much of the technology we now take for granted was birthed and improved with the threat of failure hanging dangerously close, yet scientists and engineers persisted. It would seem that all inventors and investors are trained as fear-killers, overpowering the enemy of their dreams to go on to the most marvellous innovations.

Failure doesn't threaten their self-confidence. Being wrong doesn't make them feel stupid. They have adopted a perspective that reaffirms their intellect and talent even in the face of defeat. They know that no matter how many times they experience failure, they are not themselves "a failure". In fact, the more successful someone becomes the more eager they seem to run into circumstances that have a considerable risk of failure. Steve Jobs, Bill Gates and Elon Musk all prove the hypothesis that if you play big, you fail big and win even bigger. By observing the lives of the real risk takers and fear killers I have come to discover a powerful truth. Let's call it Tomlinson's Law. It is simply this - to attain high levels of success we must welcome the reality of high rates of failure.

We have given failure such a poor reputation that people avoid it when they should run right through it. It seems to be the constant fuel that propels the most successful among us. People see failure as a flaw, when losing in the pursuit of a thing is not failure. The failure lies in thinking that a loss makes you a life-long loser. Losing a house, job or a spouse is enough for some to think that they are on the wrong side of luck and their fate will only get worse. They submit a resignation letter to Executive Director Fear and walk away. Fear wins.

In 2012 I was a final year student at the University of the West Indies. I had just finished serving two years as part of the Guild of Students - the student governance body on the campus. As I was exiting my role as Vice President, a long-standing matter was raised among our executive that we felt needed urgent attention before the year ended. Students who had not completed payment of their school fees or boarding fees would be prevented from sitting their examinations and would also receive a failing grade for all subjects they were registered for. This entire process was known as de-registration. The Guild felt the policy was unjust as it meted out a double-penalty to students who were financially vulnerable. The problem, we thought, was two-fold. First, they would not be able to sit the exams because of their financial challenges which meant spending an extra Semester in University (an added expense for the already poor) and, secondly, receiving an automatic F for all subjects meant they had no chance of ever applying for a scholarship to help offset those costs in the new Semester (one less option for the already poor).

We petitioned the administration, sought meetings, negotiated a suspension of the policy, but the answer was always no. The University had its bills to pay, the subvention from central government was not forthcoming and students needed to take full responsibility for their education was the line we were fed. But we wouldn't bite. On the first day of final examinations we organised a protest demanding that the Ministry of Education intervene and that the University exercise some discretion on behalf of the students. Our protest moved from the front gate of the University to the main examination centre where protesters overturned desks, tore up examination papers and disrupted examinations while singing the national anthem.

The end result? All students were able to sit their examinations and today the de-registration process no longer involves an automatic F for failing to pay all fees in time for examinations. As the chief ring-leader however, my fate would not be so glorious. I was suspended from all student activities which meant I could no longer represent the University in debating, nor could I hold a position of leadership. Having just been selected to serve as a Resident Adviser I was asked to vacate my lodging on campus. If it ended there I could've handled it but it got worse. I was a national headline. Television, radio and print stories were carried identifying me as a reckless, impetuous hothead who had no place leading a herd of cows, much less a student body. Not only was I stripped of the respect and status I had earned on campus over the three years, I was now being publicly reprimanded by an entire nation. The only comfort, if one could call it that, was to know I wasn't alone. Two of my fellow rebels were suffering a similar fate and so we had each other's company during our lamentations.

This was a national disgrace and a permanently recorded failure. Unlike many others who get to fail quietly in their homes, workplaces or in front of a small crowd, I failed for an entire country to see.

To date, I consider this my biggest, scariest experience with failure because of the magnitude of the backlash. At age 22, my life flashed before my eyes and it all went dark. It took almost a year for me to be able to speak about the incident without stuttering or feeling my heart drop to my small intestines. That one incident had me convinced that I was bound to become a failure. There was no way I could rescue my reputation after this. I was wrong.

I remember a conversation with my mother during the heights of public commentary. She had heard an interview where the Minister of Education and a prominent journalist took issue with my character as a leader for supporting this kind of action.

"Krystal, I don't know what's going to happen. This country is so small and if the Government blacklists you, who will employ you? You embarrassed the Minister and he might never forget this," she said. I could hear the worry in her voice and I know she honestly believed that I would have to move to another country to get a clean start. I thought so, too. We were wrong.

This big flop taught me lessons and sharpened me in ways I could not have known were necessary. I would do it again (thank goodness I don't have to) because it set me up for a new brand of resilience. If I didn't die after millions saw me fail then what is there to be afraid of?
I came out of that experience with 2 big lessons that I have carried with me ever since.

1. The fact that you're doing the right thing is no guarantee that things will come out right. Still do the right thing
2. People love a great comeback, so come back. Let the past pass and come back to NOW.

Kill Fear

I eventually started my Masters programme at the same University, was re-engaged with a contract, served 2 years as a Resident Advisor and have been invited back on several occasions to speak at University functions as an outstanding Pelican (our school mascot is the Pelican).

Failure is a test of resilience. It is a question from the universe, inquiring just how badly you want something and how hard you are willing to push for it. When we fear failure more than we trust our resilience we answer the universe's question with a NO.

Every time we hand in our drive, passion, discipline and resilience - *fear wins*. And when fear wins, you lose.

This fear of failure is linked to a sense of vulnerability. The belief that we are somehow weakened in social standing if we are wrong about something or fail to get the perfect results from our efforts. That is the way of human experience. There are no guarantees, but there are always opportunities to apply the lesson of a past failure to improve future effort.

I conducted an impromptu poll online and was not surprised to find that the most common fear among my audience was a fear of failure. In a society that has made knowledge gathering and sharing so effortless, it is understandable that people feel pressured, now more than ever, to be massively successful, quickly and consistently. We watch as our peers fly across the world, secure big promotions, buy flashy cars, marry models and moguls and have magazine-ready babies, and become acutely aware of how single, broke and professionally unfulfilled we are. Our perceived lack of progress is amplified by the emotional tax we pay every time we peep into other people's lives. Stop the endless comparison and digital competition and decide whether you are willing to do what they have done to get where they have gotten. And that includes a healthy dose of failure.

Living fearlessly demands change. We can no longer comply with the coward within. You must be prepared to take some risks and experience failure. It is true to think that nothing tried, nothing failed, but it is also true that nothing tried, nothing gained. If you never want the feeling of failure, do nothing. You are safe in that state of immobility. You will be safe from change, challenge, trials and triumph. There is no loss, nor is there any meaningful win available in that dark corner filled with the shadows of dreams unexplored. So as you decide to avoid the losses, know too that you are forfeiting your wins.

In fact, we should hurry up and fail. Fail now, win later. I am convinced that no matter what the outcome, win or lose, it will not define me. Here is a statement I repeat often and with sincerity. It is part of my belief system and encourages me to do more and fear less.

I am not a failure. I experience failure. I am not a success. I experience success. I am defined only by my potential which is immeasurable and cannot be contained.

Whenever an outcome discourages me, I encourage myself with this statement. Whenever an outcome excites me, I tame my ego with this statement. This affirmation keeps me grounded while in motion. It helps me to build momentum and it delivers deadly poison to the fear of failure.

Remind yourself at every juncture that you have the power to do better every day, even after your worst days. It is the greatest disservice to your potential when you attempt to walk into your future with the baggage of who you used to be instead of the power of your potential. Allow your past to pass. Take the lessons and apply them quickly, but leave the load where it belongs - behind you.

Always work in the now. Come here. Get out of every other reality and come HERE. Dedicate your awareness to the present moment. Stop ruminating in past experiences and stop cultivating anxiety with an obsession with what might go wrong in the future. Come into NOW. How are you now? Where are you now? What are you capable of now?

Work in your *now.*

You don't need to remind yourself of all the things you got wrong before. Dale Carnegie in his hallmark writing on how to influence others shared a very telling couplet that is useful to place here. It goes, *once I did bad and that I heard ever. Twice I did good and that I heard never.*

The world does not need your help to hold you back. It can do it on its own with the nay-sayers and the former friends who wish you walls and barriers instead of bridges and clear paths. Don't volunteer your time and energy to the destruction of your self-esteem. Just as you are preparing to turn a corner and become a better version of you, the frequency of "used" to will get louder in your environment. Your old and new colleagues, friends and family will be eager to remind you of who you used to be and what you used to do and what you never had and why you don't deserve more. They will speak loudly - to those who care and to those who don't. You must have a voice louder than theirs that speaks the truth about who you can become, that progress and growth are your right as a child of the universe.

Never wait on the world to celebrate your talent when they are busy trying to find out if they have any of their own. Don't wait to have your unique mind and heart validated by those who are still constrained by the opinions of others.

Can I start over?

Clarity gives you purpose and that is the only thing that will set you straight when fear wants to lead you astray. It is the most important vaccination against the infection that stymies your entry into the arena of excellence and high performance. Get clear on your reason to succeed and get clear early. While there is no late entry into the game of self-awareness, the sooner you get glued to a bolder and brighter vision for your life, the sooner you can enjoy the gains and the successes. But if you don't know what you're digging for, how will you know when you've struck gold? Only clarity helps you to identify and measure your success and only clarity gives fear the taser-like jolt to back down when you are looking to step up.

Clarity is not so much centred on the "what" in your goals but the "why". When your why is strong enough, fear is no match for that intensity. My teenage years offered me much clarity on my "why" even before I understood the "what" and the "how". I vividly remember the moment I chose to shift gears from mediocre to excellent. I was standing on the corridor on my high school campus waiting for my mother to exit the principal's office. I had graduated earlier that year from the 11th grade and the custom in Jamaica is to reapply after graduation to complete the 12th and 13th grades - or 6th Form, our proper title.

My external examination grades had come in and I had passed all the subjects I sat. For one of them, I did so well that I was ranked first in the country. I was 16 years old, doing well with little effort and hoping to cruise through the next couple of years as I had done for the last 5. I was in for a rude awakening.

My mother exited the office after about ten minutes with a mixed look of disappointment and contained anger. I knew exactly what had happened. The principal had said no to my being readmitted to the school. When she confirmed my suspicion I felt a wave of sadness, not because of that instant rejection, but that my mother had to be my proxy. She was dealt the blow on my behalf.

She was told that I was not a suitable candidate even though my grades met the stated requirement. My behaviour excluded me from consideration. I was a miscreant. I'll be the first to tell you that the composed young woman I am today is nothing like that teenage tyrant that walked the corridors of my high school. I was not surprised that the principal chose to turn me away, but I was hurt. I was hurt because it was a moment of embarrassment for my mother who did not deserve to have a door closed in her face or a request denied simply because I was undisciplined. I didn't show it at the time but I was furious and ashamed. I was accepted by another institution after making myself a silent promise.

If this school will accept me so I can make a fresh start, I will change my entire approach. I will be so good that my name no longer shuts, but opens doors for my mother.

What I was looking dead in the eyes was change, and that made me very, very afraid.

Change is hard work. It's hard to accept, understand and live with even though it is a constant reality for each of us. We cherish the sameness of things. We love customs and traditions, patterns and habits. They are reliable and sure. That measure of predictability puts our mind at ease because we get to operate from our basal ganglia - the neural base of operations for our habits. Once we have developed a pattern of thought or action related to our environment we stop looking for conscious ways to approach it. My favourite example of this is brushing teeth.

I remember when I was a toddler and just got the authority to brush my teeth. There were many mornings that I would forget until my mother reminded me. The "art" of brushing was difficult to conquer because each time I would forget to brush a particular area. Sometimes I wouldn't get to the molars or I'd completely forget to brush my tongue. It took so much focus and attention and if I got distracted by even a thought, the entire process was wrecked. I would even start over because I couldn't remember where in the maze I got lost.

Fast forward, decades later, to when I am now a maverick at it. I can brush my teeth without looking in the mirror and I've added a few features to the process. I text or walk to the kitchen to put eggs to boil. I go through the closet to pick my gym clothes or my jewellery drawer to properly accessorise the #OOTD (outfit of the day). Now it's not because I am a genius at mastering complexity because my math teacher could easily dismiss that assertion.

It is entirely the work of my basal ganglia which helps me create a routine that requires very little if any conscious decision making. Can you imagine what would happen if scientists discovered that we had been going about brushing all wrong? I would revert to that 6-year-old child focusing diligently, painfully on learning this new habit. Now apply that example to everything you know how to do that you now take for granted because it's ingrained. Like reading and writing from left to right, driving on a particular side of the road, walking one foot in front of the next. What if the rules changed when you woke up tomorrow and you had to now write from right to left or drive on the opposite side of the road or walk one foot behind the next? Just the thought makes me a little anxious. All that re-learning is intimidating and that's precisely the reason we shy away from change, particularly when it is forced upon us. It requires new learning and that demands the commitment of energy and focus. We fear those long hours of ignorance before we become masters at a new pursuit. We fear the awkward, embarrassing and frustrating moments that are sure to come.

But the fear of change can be slain.

When I chose to change at age 16, I wasn't sure how I would get that done or exactly what the end result would look like. But despite the fear of changing schools, friends and attitude I had a powerful weapon, one that I would sharpen for bigger goals in time to come. That weapon was my purpose.

The power of my why, my reason, was so great that no measure of uncertainty could deter me. My mother and her reputation became my all-important WHY.

I made a 180 degree turn at a time when it would have been much easier to allow my hormones to lead me. I developed a passion for leadership, debate and public speaking that truly gave me a new sense of self and laid the foundation for me to build a reputation that could work for me and my family and not against us. This only happened because I found a great big reason to change. I saw the reward that my mother would be able to reap if I started to do things differently and that garroted my fear.

These days, my mom enjoys introducing herself to others as Krystal's mom, as it should be. My purpose led me to take the high road, even as the low road enticed me. My why outweighed my 'whatever, it doesn't matter' and I moved in the direction of my legacy and not my lazy. I slipped quite a few times but those moments were never allowed to define me. The fear and self-doubt that stealthily stalked me have learnt not to challenge what Darren Hardy refers to as my "why-power". It will always lose. The fact that fear has more than nine lives doesn't make me any less eager to kill it whenever it presents itself.

When you call on the power of purpose not even the fear of death is enough to interrupt your momentum.

When the reason is unreasonably compelling, we conjure up the courage to act with scant regard for all the things that could go wrong. What will be your "why"? Is it your child, your health, your peace of mind, your parents? The desire to be successful is not enough if money is the primary payoff. You must be driven by a deeper calling that lights a fire in your gut. The kind that will keep you up at nights and wake you early each morning. That "why" is your way to a fulfilling win.

Kill Fear

On Friday September 8, 2017, in Jamaica, just 4 days into the start of the new school term, a 12-year old boy was walking with a group of friends on the way home from school. It was raining heavily and a nearby gully was flooded. The boy, encouraged by his friends, jumped into the gully and was washed away by the violent current of the water. As residents in the community looked at one man jumped in after the youngster and ended up saving the boy's life. Was he a trained lifeguard? No. He was a man whose purpose killed his fear.

What can you tell yourself to get on the court while the crowd stares, jeers and with phone cameras ready to capture every moment? You have a big idea, you want to take a risk on your passion, you're ready to do things differently but you can't see the full picture. How do you move? How do you kill fear?

HOW TO FIRE

Fortis Cadere...

You are not called to perfection. Start by reminding yourself that you are human and you have a right to your mistakes. Recall a great revelation that came because you blundered. Think of your biggest failure to date and then feel for your pulse.
YOU SURVIVED!

Chances are, you broke no bones and lost no blood in this big, scary experience with failure. Your ego just took a hit. But yet, here you are; breathing, laughing, moving, and living. You survived.

There is a famous school motto in my country that reflects this truth that even when we are struck down, we don't have to die.

Fortis cadere, cedere non potest - The brave may fall but never yield.

There are two popular definitions of the word "may". One speaks to the possibility that a thing might happen. So you may read the above to say that it is possible for the brave to fall.

The other definition is that of asking or receiving permission in which case you would read the above to say the brave have permission to fall. I choose the latter. Give yourself permission to fall. It is proof that you are moving. And it's highly preferred that you fall on your face. That's a guarantee that even in the loss of poise and balance you are now further ahead than when you were standing.

None of us will ever know what the end looks like when we begin. We must relinquish the need to control our circumstance and embrace the power we have to control our response to them. The world does not owe us a hurdle-free journey to our destinies. Once we get comfortable with the idea that things will fall apart despite our greatest planning and efforts we diminish that fear of "what next". The unknown is scary because we fear the let-down. We fail to give credit to the hard blows that open us up to new knowledge and renewed vigour. If life was a sure shot with all outcomes good and sure, how would you find happiness?

I have come to relate my happiness with problems. For every problem that I have solved I leave feeling stronger, smarter and bolder. With no problems to solve how would I test my strength and wisdom? If all the answers were already laid before me I would hardly be able to use this beautiful mind. We need problems. They are our pathways to victory. We need uncertainty. It is the prerequisite for courage.

So what if you stumble? It's proof that you're moving! Let no moss gather and smother your potential. Be still for a season and then take action. Move, grow, fail, learn and Kill fear with the truth that you are human and it is the way of humanity to err. It gives character to every success story to know that there were trials and errors. The truth is you have been equipped to deal with failure, having failed quite a bit in the past. We all have, and most will tell you they are better for it.

Speak the truth to yourself about what failure in a particular arena will cost you, but balance it with the truth of what you stand to gain.

Purpose

Find a reason bigger than yourself and use it to propel you into doing whatever seems new and unconquerable. When you discover purpose your approach to life will be forever transformed. Purpose is not a mystical, fleeting idea or emotion. It is a very tangible thing. Purpose comes from a sense of clarity on who you want to become and why you want to become that person. Purpose means you begin to act from a place of conscious decision-making and not allowing habits or fear to lead you. Purpose is control. Control of thoughts, words and actions. Purpose will stretch you and cultivate discipline in areas of your life you thought were too far gone to recover.

Your purpose is not likely to be something cosmetic and external like changing people's lives or ending poverty. It develops once you have clarified the truth of who will be and not necessarily what you will do. Start with a vision of what your best **self** should look like and not what your best **assets** should look like. I envision my best self being compassionate, honest and constantly investing in my professional development and personal relationships. Will that lead to personal and professional excellence? Undoubtedly. But to start with the end in mind means that I am depending others to recognise and validate me - a variable I have no control over and one that might generate fear of what is unknown, for example how people will feel about me. Shift focus from trying to guarantee outputs to mastering the quality of inputs.

Your purpose and vision don't have to remain static either. They can change and that is absolutely fine. My why at age 16 was not my why at age 25 and my why today is different too. I expect my purpose at age 50 will also be different. Our reason for pushing beyond our limits and rising above our circumstances will differ and may even be propelled by less than noble outcomes, such as revenge, but we can all come up with a why. The more meaningful your why, the greater power it has to castrate any ounce of fear that keeps your passions and dreams comatose. Your ascension to new levels of contribution is awaiting that fuel, and guess what? It's something you can give yourself. It matters not whether you are born with it or if it took a period of distress to help you craft it, once you have it, it's yours and it will do for you what years of self-pity and procrastination could not.

When I am faced with any shift in my personal, professional or financial life I also tune into the truth of my dynamism. It's part of my self-defined identity. We all have that power to be dynamic instead of dormant.

Welcome change. Remain buoyant and ready to progress. A dynamic approach to life includes these qualities. Learn to ride the waves instead of fighting the flood of the unexpected and unfamiliar. Test the entrepreneur within you and begin to find opportunity within the chaos of life. Trust yourself to be able to conquer whatever hurdles life presents and find courage in the fact that many have faced the same struggles or worse, and did not drown in the despair, but chose to rise in resolve and optimism.

Because we are not yet able to guarantee outcomes and see what comes next, it is a better use of our imagination to believe that we are competent enough to conquer the next chapter. Remember, your belief about who you are and what you have the potential to do will design a lens for your life.

When you know your "why" the "what ifs" don't matter.

Plan the trip up

That fear of failure is made possible by a sense that anything can happen and we might not be prepared. So prepare.

Find a mentor who has walked the path. Plant your feet in the kind of soil that supports and nourishes your spirit.

Set value based goals instead of output based ambitions so you can celebrate your effort even if the outcome isn't perfect. In my example, the value based goal was to commit my best effort to advocate on behalf of the student body at my alma mater, not to stage a successful protest. I could count it a success because I did my best. Today I would do better but back then, that was my best.

Finally, be honest about what you want for dinner and do not be compelled to want what everyone else is having. Your desire for success must be yours. In stimulating that desire, be honest. Know whether you are capable of doing a thing, not whether everyone else is. Assess how committed you will be to learning how to do a thing right. Don't jump blindly into the sea and think you can pretend your way into staying afloat. Are you a swimmer? Will you need a life vest? Will you need a lifeguard on duty? Be honest about your strength and limitations and what skills you will need to get started. You don't need the whole toolkit from A-Z, only enough to get started, and a mind keen and humble enough to keep learning.

Plan the trip up.

CHAPTER FIVE
CRITICISM

The most challenging feature of the 21st Century technology shift on people's psyche is that we must now countenance the views of others on our lives. Those comment bars on Instagram, Facebook, and Twitter open us up to a barrage of criticisms and opinions from people who don't even know who we are. Their words can be vicious, disrespectful, and even untrue; but worse yet, they are there for all to see.

When we stand and observe, critique, and cajole others as they make an attempt at fulfilling their dreams, we remind ourselves why we don't pursue ours to begin with. We say about others the things we are afraid they will say about us. Knowing what we do and say when others around us are stepping boldly into a new foray, we cringe at the thought of doing anything similar. We are truly our worst enemies. The next time you hear someone shining a negative light on someone else's attempt at a new personal or professional pursuit take the time to think, how is the critic living their own life? Are they taking any risks? Are they living with a sense of purpose? Are they seeking to challenge themselves in the way the subject of their criticism is?
Before you cower in fear of the opinions of strangers who care little about whether you fail or succeed, get some clarity. It is the best defence against useless chatter and crushing critique.

F.O.P.O. - Fear of People's Opinions

"Allodoxaphobia" is the fear of hearing what others think about us. Even if we were never frightened by the opinions of strangers, technology now brings it to our feet. In a vibrantly opinionated world, we are assaulted by the thoughts of other people at the most inopportune time. We never ask for it, but strangers are lurking online waiting for the perfect opportunity to say what they think about your hair, your clothes, your spouse or your performance, whether or not you are a public figure. This overload of opinion has forced many bright lights into the shadows for fear that someone might say something, true or untrue, that cuts deeply at their core. The allodoxaphobic are withdrawn, reserved, shy and often looking to sit as far away from the limelight as possible. They may be busy trying to do things how everyone else does just to fit in and diminish the likelihood that they will be noticed or called to the front. These are not habits that lead to excellence or outstanding achievement. If you decide to be held captive by this fear of what others might say then you have forgone the fruits of your potential. Every time you allow someone to set limits for you with their opinions you give them the keys to drive you crazy.

Perhaps it wouldn't be so bad if people were unkind privately, but the added feature of having those comments seen by yet more strangers amplifies the frequency of fear. This is a rational response and is not proof that you are weak.

When we feel threatened our fight or flight mechanisms in our body get activated. This threat doesn't have to be physical or immediate, it need only be perceived as possibly causing us harm. As social creatures who depend on human relationships and acceptance to create our identity, a public attack on who we are threatens our space in society. Our body will have a physiological response to prepare us to fight or to run, but we are sitting at the dinner table with our phones in our hands. We can really take no action.

Or can we?

Even outside of the digital space we have to deal with stinging criticism from people we know, love, and trust. That can be the most frustrating because we are already vulnerable with and connected to them. Our fear of the opinions of family members and friends keeps us miserably trapped in relationships that have outlived their meaning; jobs that lack fulfilment, degree programmes that fail to stimulate, churches that don't align with our deepest beliefs on life and the Creator. We live below the joy radar just so people will say nice things about us.

This opinion fear must be cut off at the root and that only happens when you learn to deafen your ear to the things that are not goal-relevant. One of the questions that I am often asked is how I maintain a positive attitude and a kind spirit even in the midst of scalding public criticism and ridicule. My answer is always that I am deaf to all things emotionally destructive. I take advice from persons who give it from a place of love. And you'll know which pieces of criticism come from a soul meant to refresh yours. That critique comes through a conversation, not as a passing comment on Instagram or Facebook, and it also comes with a few suggestions on how to get it right the next time. It's not always packaged with kisses and hugs, but the quality of the gift is unquestionable.

All other opinions get returned to the sender, unopened. How often do you open those packages meant to burn your eyes and send darts straight to your soul? Even more telling, how often do you go looking for them? Scouring the comment section, polling friends to see if anyone has said something you don't like? You must choose what you want to find and feel and look exclusively for those. It is a fine act of self-betrayal to say you want to live a life guided by superior thoughts while simultaneously searching the gutters for negative ones.

When you pay attention to something, it costs you. Attention paid to one thing means that another thing has been denied your focus. The human mind is able to keep ONLY ONE THING in conscious awareness at a time. So while we can rapidly alter our focus we cannot multi-focus.

What have you chosen to be consciously aware of?

When it comes to opinions, learn to deposit your finite focus into opinions, whether positive or negative, that are goal-relevant. A track and field athlete being criticised for poor posture in the blocks or his slow response time to the gun would do well to pay attention to the criticism. His goal is to improve his performance on the track. Critique about his efforts on the track are goal-relevant. He will have to choose to ignore the comments about his skin colour, acne, and crooked teeth. None of those are goal-relevant. He is not aiming to be a Sports Illustrated model or Colgate ambassador.

A woman who is managing a restaurant must tune in to the criticism from customers on the quality of service, food, and ambiance. Her goal is to provide a positive culinary experience for her guests. Those criticisms are goal-relevant. Negative comments on her hair cut, the fact that she is still single with no children, or the absence of a thigh-gap will have to be ignored because they don't help her to achieve her goal, but will certainly steal her focus and water her fear of people's opinions.

It may sound odd but it is very possible to actively filter what you hear in your environment. You are already doing it unconsciously. We apply listening filters every second of the day. Our beliefs and cognitive constraints determine how we hear. If we think we are insignificant we will listen for proof that matches that belief. However, the woman who thinks she is brilliant and beautiful shows up in the world looking for proof of that. Depending on what you believe about yourself you will see, hear, and feel all the stimuli that feed into that faith. Those are food for your spirit and you will not go a day without that spiritual food. You will call the friend who often reminds you of what you believe about you. You will log on and visit the social media accounts that reflect the truth you hold about you. You will stay in that intimate relationship that affirms the truth about you. Whether that is good or bad, it feeds your inner belief and you will remain loyal to that tree and its fruits.

Think of the most successful person in your life, the person who is happiest, kindest, and most often at peace in their relationship or job. Now, think of someone who is the complete opposite; always anxious, incorrigible, pessimistic, and tired. Do these two persons have the same friends? Do they enjoy the same activities in their past time? Do they speak and laugh about the same topics? Do they have the same daily habits? In other words, do they feed from the same fruit trees?

The answer is probably "no". Their diet is different which explains why their health in the personal and professional realms does not align. So what trees do you feed from? Who do you align yourself with? What is your state of emotional health how can you improve your diet to revitalise your spirit?

No one can answer that for you. Only you can assess the state of your relationships and wellbeing and decide which roots to cut and which branches to prune. Your life depends on you taking action. Not as a victim or casualty, but as the CEO.

When you have faith in your ability to make the bold and daring choices that match your confidence, you diminish the fear of what people will say about those choices. When you return the authority to choose to the real owner of your life - YOU - then the outcomes begin to differ. You must exercise the power you have to choose. You can choose how you feel. You can choose what you hear. You can choose how to use what you hear and feel and act in a way that affirms the belief you have of yourself. More powerful than that, you can choose new beliefs about yourself. You are not committed eternally to who you were yesterday. If that is not the best version of you, then you can manifest a better one.

I remember battling with a deeply personal decision in February of 2016 and the fight was really a FOPO fight. By then I had been dating my current partner for three months and the story was about to hit the front page of a national tabloid. I nearly died from fear! I had started a new job in a high profile corporate company, my family was still not comfortable with the news of who I was dating, and I was just not prepared to have people's eyes and ears all over my personal relationship. I sat up the entire night playing with the scenarios of what people would think and what it would cost me; my job, my privacy, my relationships with family and friends - and in no scenario did I come out better off. Fear took my appetite, my focus, my peace and I started to feel like I had committed a crime and was now going on trial. Can you imagine feeling like a criminal for doing what everyone else has the right to do - just love someone?

It was prison. An entire week of feeling like a prisoner because people didn't agree with who I chose to love.

The story was published and the opinions rolled in. And life went on. Now, three years into the relationship, many more stories have been published and I am no worse off than I was before. All the opinions that I feared came and went but I soon realised that they had no power. I didn't lose my job or anything else I expected to lose because people's opinions don't have that kind of influence over my success. People's opinions don't have the authority over my life.

I left that prison the moment I realised that my love life didn't come with a permission slip. No one needed to sign it to approve my decisions as an adult. I did not need the validation of another human being. To be honest, I have never needed it but when people start to give you large doses of what you don't need you will start to believe that it is necessary. I got to a state of what Jamaicans call "doh cya" which is an adjective in our patios derived from the English phrase "don't care". My doh cya has been so liberating. I accepted two truths in this period of distress:

1. Everyone has a right to their opinion
2. I have the right not to care about them.

I am bolder, braver and more successful for it. I have built a relationship with a man who has never betrayed my trust, treats me like the most important person in the world, shows up for me physically and emotionally, and drops his guard to allow me to support and strengthen him, while he does the same for me. He offers me emotional security, loyalty, and respect that I would never trade for the opinions of others.

Kill Fear

If you can purge yourself of the unhealthy thoughts, conversations, and relationships that keep derailing you and pointing you away from your highest level of contribution then you begin to heal your spirit and make room for the blossoming and blooming that you deserve. Don't be deceived by fear. Don't be disarmed by the feeling of comfort as you rest on your laurels and lower your standards to fit in. It has never been worth it. I know of no man or woman who boasts of the fruits of underachievement and conformity and that is simply because there are no fruits worth boasting about.

Don't watch the crowd; their duty is to be loud. Believe in what you're doing and feel proud. These are lines from one of my personal anthems. It is a song titled "Warriors don't cry" by Beres Hammond, a prolific Jamaican reggae singer. It is a song that testifies to the need for fixity of purpose and a deep understanding of spectators. They will cheer, boo, jeer, and commend you, but they offer no advice on how you can grow. That is not their job. They do not come to the stands with a zest to nourish your spirit. Their duty is simply to be loud. Will you stay down for fear of the crowd in the stands or be empowered by a personal commitment to always get on the track and move?

Our children are the most fearless among us and that is because they have not yet learned how to fear people and opinions. Observe a child and you are bound to appreciate their boldness and unabashed pursuit for more. I have had the blessing of helping to watch and care for a baby and some of my best life lessons came through that experience. I was 11 years old when my cousin was born. I did the babysitting, diaper changing, and feeding rituals and got to see her grow into a very self-assured young woman. I remember when she was just learning to walk and on some days I allowed my own fear of what might go wrong to keep her strapped into her high chair or in her crib.

She would struggle to stand and topple over, or bump into furniture earning her fair share of blotches and bruises. But she was never deterred. She failed in private, she failed in public, and never stopped trying to walk. She failed in front of family members and strangers and carried all the scars to prove it but she never stopped trying to walk. She teetered and fumbled awkwardly in the home, through supermarket aisles, and on the beach but she never stopped trying. At no point did she think that because she didn't look right doing it she should stop. No matter how we 'big people' chuckled at her failed attempts, there was no shame or fear of failing in front of us. She fell in the most graceless ways and floundered to get back up, sometimes needing our help to do so, but not once did she doubt her ability to get it right even when we projected our fears on her.

Today she is a dancer and walks quite fine.

Her story is not unique. Every single one of us was once that fearless baby, failing for all to see, but never doubting our ability to get it right. Never becoming preoccupied with people's opinions of what we could or could not do. What others thought hardly mattered, what they said mattered even less. It was as if we perfected our "doh cya" before we knew what it was.

So, who taught us to fear what others think? When did opinions start to matter more than our ambitions? We might not know who or when but what is sure is that it was not of our own doing.

We were born fearless.

HOW TO FIRE

Reveal your humanity

There are days when I want to return to my childlike self where I was numb to the opinions of others and imbued with an intractable focus on my goals. On those days I channel my youngest self. Some people have a game face but I have a baby face where I return to my nascent stage of mental cleanliness before people corrupted my view of the world and diminished pieces of my confidence and ask "what would the baby do about this goal?" The answer is always: she would keep trying. Amidst the noise and naysayers, she would keep trying! I am not pretending to be anyone but me. The original me who did not feel compelled to colour within the lines and stop because someone said so. That first me…that bold, daring me. And so, with knowledge of who I originally am, I kill fear. At the heart of it I am saying to the world that I embrace my imperfect effort. Yes, I will give you something to criticise, but keep watching. You will inevitably see me get it right.

Much like failure is part of the human experience, having that failure criticised is also part of the journey.

Every time I choose vulnerability it is a conscious decision to accept my own imperfections and maintain a learning posture. I don't know it all or have it all and that is not my duty as a human being. I choose to be human, which means changing my unreasonable expectation to be alright all the time and fly in fine style. I choose to be human and make my mistakes and talk about them with other humans who may wish to learn some lessons without the fatigue of the journey I endured. I accept that being human subtly and gregariously gives other humans permission to be the same.

And that is absolutely FINE.

One of the first things that we sacrifice when we allow the fear of appearing human and exposing our vulnerability to lead us is our love life, and the ability to truly build an intimate partnership with someone else. We have a unique desire for pair-bonding but not many of us understand how to build a strong bond with our mates. It is through emotional disclosure.

When couples become trusting of each other, partners begin to share their deepest and most painful scars. By sharing this experience of pain and suffering, they weave a solid fabric of connectedness that stands the test of time even after the raw desire and sexual fever have abated. Think about the person you are closest to and the circumstances that led to such a deep connection. Was it a pain-based experience? Did it require one or both of you to be vulnerable? When we choose to be emotionally impenetrable and show no weakness we allow that fear of someone abusing our tender humanity to prevent a noble heart from loving that very thing. If you are having a difficulty building new and meaningful friendships, assess how human you are in those spaces. Are you giving people permission or opportunity to touch your humanity?

If you are having difficulty building a strong emotional connection with your intimate partner, assess how vulnerable you are allowing yourself to be. Look at how vulnerable they are with you. Disclosure is a cornerstone of trust. Instead of wondering how weak you will appear and fearing the judgement of mortals, consider the more profound benefit of having a **"real-ationship"**.

If we can accept our blemish-filled lives and celebrate the valley-riddled journey it gives us great perspective on our resilience and never-ending capacity to learn and grow at every hurdle. Instead of sitting in shame and personifying our defeat we can choose to use them as tools to deepen our connection with others and add immeasurable value to relationships. With that kind of experience in our personal space, the public pressure for perfection becomes a walk in the park.

The unfortunate truth is that so many humans need machines to help them mimic relationships and social media is the purest demonstration of how our need for social connectedness can be warped into something unhealthy and unreal.

Kim Kardashian seems to be making it difficult for wives everywhere. The body, the business, the beauty seems too much to compete with, especially if you don't have a bank account to sustain the pursuit. When Alicia Keys stopped wearing makeup I found it so refreshing. A beautiful and talented black woman decided that as she was, she was enough. It's almost tragic that we have to celebrate people just for being who they are, but such is the world today. Who you are seems to be of little value compared to how you look and that makes it less attractive and socially acceptable to be authentic.

Paradoxically, it has never been more important that we display our authentic selves. Believing that who we are is just not enough, we have started setting standards and raising bars that do not naturally exist and experience deep resentment for others and personal dissatisfaction when we are unable to do the unreasonable thing. It's exhausting, this grand show of perfection. And it is the source of all sorts of envy and hate, this perfect life that really does not exist.

So, when Alicia Keys stopped wearing makeup it was a major victory for women everywhere who felt pressured to spend thousands of dollars to hide our blemishes and say we woke up flawless. This culture of celebrating perfection slowly erodes our humanity and makes us feel less comfortable displaying it.

We don't talk about the struggle but we broadcast the shine. We put a filter over the pain and hashtag our gains. There is no space to fail in excellence and no room for vulnerability in a strong man or woman…right? WRONG.

Experiential Diversity

"Variety's the very spice of life, that gives it all its flavour" ~ William Cowper, The Task (1785)

That quote has been expressed in varied ways but almost always to refer to sexual conquest, new beginnings, weather, and changes in personal taste. I have yet to see it used to contextualise our life's most difficult moments. Somehow the spice is poison when it does not come with a clear silver lining. But even in struggle, this principle has merit. Our life could not be meaningful if all we registered were wins and successes. In the same way, psychologists encourage our emotional diversity - experiencing and sitting with our feelings of joy, anger, excitement and anxiety - so we can learn the lessons of the emotional season. We must also embrace our flaws and failures as part of this distinct human journey.

While we may not want strangers to have intimate knowledge of our moments of profound self-doubt, insecurities, and ignorance, we must be cautious that in hiding from others we do not hide from ourselves.

We must also pull back these protective and perfectionist veils to allow others who love and value us to help. If no one knows you are in trouble, how can they be of much help? Build safe spaces within your friendships that allow vulnerability and candid expression of hurt and disappointment. To build real trust and friendship there needs to be nakedness between the parties involved.

Your intimate partner does not need to see you naked for intercourse to take place, but eventually we get to a point where the misappropriated fat, dark spots and stretch marks form part of our beauty instead of a tool of ridicule. We get comfortable with our imperfect physique being seen by another person because we trust that they see us as more than flesh and bones, that our value transcends what we look like.

The same is required by and from our friends. Before we get comfortable sharing painful truths with strangers we must find security and trust within our network of friends. Though easier said than done, it is not impossible and should be a priority as we build our networks and pursue joy and belonging among peers.

This fear that if we reveal our humanity it makes us less powerful and strips us of respect is a mass-peddled falsehood that needs to die first in our personal and intimate relationships and eventually across our social landscape. If you have a friend who you feel uncomfortable sharing your failures and personal struggles with, feel the need to play perfect and together for, you do not have a friend. You are not a machine and your humanity is contained in your ability to fully experience seasons - from the flourish of spring to the barren winter times.

Many a kind word, helping hand or job recommendation have passed us by because we wear the bravado of "I got this. I don't need anyone but me". In our effort to not show weakness we miss opportunities to link into the grand web of collaborative strength. Fear locks us out of the benefit of community

In a powerful interview with Brene Brown, Viola Davis shared a thought that could well be called 21st Century gospel as we seek the salvation of true human connection.

"They tell you to develop a thick skin so things don't get to you. What they don't tell you is that your thick skin will keep everything from getting out, too. Love, intimacy, vulnerability. Thick skin doesn't work for me anymore. I will be transparent and translucent." (Brown, 2017)

We never truly connect with others if our relationships are constructed entirely on the frolic and good times. It is the display of our whole truth which inevitably includes pain, sadness, grief, and regret, and that connects us authentically. So whoever you are connected to, with only the glue of your highs, count that as superficial and strengthen it by asking for help. You can test the level of commitment and care based on how willing the other person is to help you when you need it.

Emotional Hygiene

But on the days when my "me-ness" is just not enough, I dig deeper still. While I'm filtering the noise and discarding the lies that are trying to take up space in my spirit, I also know that some noise will slither its way through the door. You should too. Don't pretend that you have a perfect defence against life. We are products of our environment and whether we choose to listen to ect defence against life. We are products of our environment and whether we choose to listen to the messages or embrace discouraging words, some things hit us when we are least prepared to put up a fight.

Even with listening filters on you will still pick up and carry negative and destructive opinions that can sink even the strongest spirit into a pit of depression. The ants will come through the cracks! We are all vulnerable and the more we pretend to be immune to constant attacks in our environment the less able we are to perform the emotional CPR that we so profoundly need.

I came upon this concept of emotional hygiene in early 2017 after watching a TEDx video presentation by Dr Guy Winch. He spoke with such clarity on how we treat emotional wounds as though they do not exist and used a powerful example that I am certain never to forget. He noted the favouritism we show for the body over the mind, sharing the story of a five-year-old who knew instinctively to reach for a Band-aid to cover the bruise. However, we don't train them to treat immediately the blows we sustain psychologically. People who express depression are told to "shake it off; it's all in your head." However someone, with a broken leg would not be told to "walk it off, it's all in your leg."(T-ED, 2015)

Because I value my mental health far more than my physical, (this is not to say I eat poorly or don't work out but I spend more hours working on my mind than I do on my body) I seek emotional healing through counselling and therapy. I accept that there are wounds I have that I am not aware of and some that I am aware of but have no idea how to correct. I also accept that my work as a mentor and personal coach puts me at risk of assimilating the hurt and fears of others by tuning in so deeply to their needs as a way of providing authentic support.

That is why I trust the doctor who has spent decades studying and practising in this area to help me clean my filters and jump back in with a renewed sense of personal power and direction. So here I am in my 20's meeting with my therapist every quarter to unravel and detangle the noise from outside that may have found its way into my psyche.

But a more consistent therapy comes from my network of friends. I have a fiercely protective and honest group of women who I lean into for support and guidance. I have found safety there. I can be vulnerable and know that it is not perceived as weakness. I can share my fears and know that no one considers me a coward but will help to retool me so I can kill it.

Find friends. Find safety in those friendships. Surround yourself with opinions you can trust, coming from people who actually care. It's not that no opinion matters. The challenge is seeking and valuing the ones that do. I have found that the "Court of Public Opinion" is always in session and ready to deliver a verdict, but that verdict is not binding. You have no obligation to live your life based on the ruling of those who do not care to know the facts of your case, the burdens you bear, and how much you have fought to come this far. You know your story and those who have helped you to rise know it too. Do not allow anyone, especially those under the cover of anonymity to set your pace and pollute your spirit with their version of how you should be living.

Self-Compassion and Forgiveness

Be honest about your flaws and release that truth into the universe. Don't spend your precious energy trying to hide behind a facade.

There is no flaw that the world can reveal about me that I haven't already revealed to myself. In recognising my own injuries, I can't be shamed by others who point it out. I am not vested in any sort of image of perfection but rather progress.

And that is the glue in the fly trap of people's opinions. We so desperately want to appear perfect that we take great offence when others remind us of our humanity. Let us put aside those Barbie/Ken aspirations and allow ourselves to become intimate with who we are and how we feel about who we are. Do not allow the great charade to destroy your greater humanity.

Despite the public veneer, we all go home to our truths. We lay down with them and rise to see them every day. We can choose to share snaps of our full existence but even if no one else knows our full story, we do. The worst person to fear is yourself. The worst person to hide from is yourself. It inevitably leads to self-destructive thoughts and behaviours in a shroud of silence, secrecy and pretend-socialisation.

What if we were to face ourselves? Not in a judgemental and self-deprecating way, pointing out our flaws and buying into people's opinions of who we should be, but in a reflective, kind and supportive way. Kristin Neff refers to it as self-compassion and it is a scientifically-tested way of killing the fear of falling short in the eyes of others and perhaps, too, ourselves. In her research, she outlines the three components of self-compassion and why it serves as a booster shot for our emotional immune system.

She defines self-compassion as the ability to silence our inner critic and replace it with a voice of kindness and comfort, speaking to ourselves as we would a friend who has made a mistake.

As self-compassionate beings, we don't validate our mistakes, but we recognise that we can't control every outcome. We are honest about our role in the conflict or disappointment and recognise that as a human being we are not alone in our suffering.

In one of her studies, Neff asked participants to record a video introduction of themselves and then told them that the video would be watched and judged by others. What she found was that those persons who ranked high on the self-compassion scale were not offended by poor feedback, while those who had scored lower found the poor feedback offensive and became defensive and aggressive. She has conducted several other experiments that prove the same point - when we learn to be compassionate to ourselves and silence our inner critic we are happier and less concerned about how people view us and measure our success.

We are all suffering. We are all struggling to make sense of our circumstances and our past. We are all in this ocean of uncertainty, working hard to ride the tide and make it to the shore. You are not alone in your suffering.

Expose yourself to the truth that all men bleed, struggle, suffer, fear, and fail just like you. The richest, brightest, most beautiful among us are still not too perfect to be human. Use the knowledge that you are not alone on this journey to give you a sense of belonging, courage, and patience as you sojourn on. Take time with you. Love you. Appreciate you and the things you have done well. And have faith in your capacity to do even better. No one knows you, like you. No one cares about your success more than you.

In The Book of Joy, the Dalai Lama and Desmond Tutu outline

eight pillars of joy, and the fifth pillar is forgiveness. In order to come to terms with our humanity, be comfortable in our own skin, and experience lasting happiness, we need to master the art of forgiveness i.e. freeing ourselves from the past. Our inability to kill the fear of this vulnerability often comes from some internally or externally inflicted wound that stays fresh in our psyche even after decades have passed.

We must forgive ourselves for the things we failed to get right. We must forgive ourselves for the limiting beliefs we have that have kept us cloaked in loneliness. Forgive ourselves for believing we couldn't do or didn't deserve something good. Forgive ourselves for forming relationships with people who undermined our better selves. Forgive ourselves for hiding in shame and in our could'ves, would'ves, should'ves. Forgive our immaturity, stubbornness and ignorance that led us into the path of wolves and snakes. We must forgive others for their betrayal and release our past pains so we can bear good fruit in the future. Without that core element of forgiveness, we never become bold enough to look fear in the face and gouge its eyes out.

My morning calibration routine includes a five-minute self-compassion exercise that reminds me to be kind to myself and not absorb the anxiety and frustrations of those around me. It also reminds me to share compassion with others who in their own struggle might be callous or unkind to me. I add this meditation as part of the coaching experience with my clients who work in high-stress environments with issues of identity and self-worth.

Self-Compassion Meditation

This meditative practice was formulated by researchers from the

Greater Good Science Centre at UC Berkeley and has proven very useful for me in my moments of suffering.

Step 1: Think of a situation in your life that is difficult and is causing you stress.

Step 2: Call the situation to mind and see if you can actually feel the stress and emotional discomfort in your body.

Step 3: Now say to yourself, "This is a moment of suffering." This acknowledgement is a form of mindfulness—of simply noticing what is going on for you emotionally in the present moment, without judging that experience as 'good' or 'bad'. You can also say to yourself, "This hurts," or, "This is stress." Use whatever statement feels most natural to you.

Step 4: Next, say to yourself, "Suffering is a part of life." This is recognition of your common humanity with others—that all people have trying experiences, and these experiences give you something in common with the rest of humanity rather than mark you as abnormal or deficient. Other options for this statement include "Other people feel this way," "I'm not alone," or "We all struggle in our lives."

Step 5: Now, put your hands over your heart, feel the warmth of your hands and the gentle touch on your chest, and say, "May I be kind to myself. May I give myself the compassion that I need. May I accept myself as I am. May I learn to accept myself as I am. May I forgive myself. May I be strong," and "May I be patient." (Greater Good Science Centre, 2015)

CHAPTER SIX
LONELINESS

We all want to fit in. It is what makes society works and social media infinitely appealing and persuasive. Human connection and relationships grease the wheels of progress and social media allows us to keep informed on the latest trends, events, fads and people. We are glued to these small screens to ensure that we don't miss out on what is trending. While that isn't inherently destructive, we put ourselves at risk of being too connected with what others are doing and eventually begin to feel that if we aren't doing it too, we are missing out on life.

F.O.M.O. - Fear of Missing Out

If we see most of our friends going off to college, we feel isolated and fear losing our connection with them, so what do we do? Start partying, whether we really want to or not. But it goes even deeper. We begin to see what people who we don't know are doing, providing more options than we can possibly pursue.

> *The first study to operationalise the concept, defined FOMO as "…the uneasy and sometimes all-consuming feeling that you're missing out – that your peers are doing, in the know about, or in possession of more or something better than you". (Przybylski, Murayama, DeHaan & Gladwell, 2013)*

The major problem with this fear is not what it stops you from doing, but what unproductive things it keeps you doing. If you are online checking your Instagram or Facebook feed almost 24/7, liking every post and almost always posting, you may have an undiagnosed fear of missing out. All the time you waste online checking on other people's lives could be better spent interrogating and improving your own.

The root cause of this fear is not ultra-sociality as we might assume. In fact, the research is quite counterintuitive. What social scientists have found is that you are "liking" other people's lives because you are unhappy. There is something unfulfilled in your own life that drives this fear of missing out. That fear pushes you online to make sure others are not doing better or that you are not doing so badly. Even if you are "liking" the posts you see and commenting with hearts and affirmations, the truth is you are only there because in your real life something is missing. You are feeling inadequate and someone else's life either helps you to forget about it or allows you to compare straws to show that yours is still taller.

If you find yourself checking your social media accounts first thing in the morning, while you eat, and just before bed, it is a strong indication that you suffer from an acute FOMO. Let's deconstruct FOMO and what it tells us about our lives (and the parts that are missing).

1. **FOMO** emerges from a sense of lack whether real or perceived. You feel that there is something you don't have, whether a healthy intimate relationship, fit physique or enough disposable income, and look to the lives of others to boost your confidence. This happens either by comparing your life to those who appear to have less than you do, based on their social media accounts, or following those who appear to have more than you do while looking for holes in their lives to prove that they are not really happy. Whether you are right or wrong, picking apart someone else's life will not help you to better construct your own.

2. FOMO is most prevalent in people who are lonely. Your overuse of social media to see and know what others are doing will not make you lonely but is likely to be proof that you lack strong human connections in your "offline" life. One study found that those who use social media more than 58 times a week are more likely to report feelings of loneliness than those who use those sites nine times for the week. (Primack, Shensa, Sidani, Whaite, Lin, Rosen, Colditz, Radovic, & Miller. 2017)

3. FOMO opens pathways to depression. This need to check in with strangers and even friends increases the likelihood, though marginally, that you will become depressed. One researcher shared, "If two women each talk to their friends for the same amount of time, but one of them spends more time reading about friends on Facebook as well, the one reading tends to grow slightly more depressed". (Marche, 2012)

FOMO, and the need to fill the gaps it reveals between our lives and theirs, is deflating. It is much like looking into your wallet after hearing how much Mark Zuckerberg made this month. Not only does it create anxiety about which event or activity you have missed but the constant check in with the lives of those around you inevitably leads to comparison. That recognition that you have less of something than someone else. The FOMO not only highlights that you are not "there" – (wherever there is) - but that you perhaps can't afford it or couldn't look as good in that crowd. You are missing more than the event but by comparison you feel as though you are missing some form of success, wellbeing and recognition.

The constant comparison is unhealthy, unfair, and unnecessary. There will always be someone better, richer, smarter, sexier, and more liked than you. In the same way you are trying to stack up with them, someone else is trying to measure up to you but you're too envious to realise what is working in your favour. We are caught in a maze of ingratitude, spinning in circles looking at what everyone has and convincing ourselves that we need it too. The time spent tipping to see over the neighbours fence could be better spent kneeling in recognition of your own gifts.

To avoid feeling as though you're left behind you end up saying yes to things you disdain, building relationships with people you dislike, and adopting values that displace your true sense of self. In your professional life you end up chasing recognition in places that give you little fulfilment and pursuing projects that mean less to you than the time you sacrifice for it.

Whatever is driving your FOMO, surrendering to it will cost you your happiness and wellbeing and nothing is worth so high a price. Your insecurities get pronounced when you are in the presence of those you think are better winners than you are and you shrink back to avoid the comparison or overcompensate to feel worthy. Neither is a healthy social response.

That is envy - the least owned feeling in the world. I have never known anyone to openly admit when they feel envious of someone else and as we watch more people reap great success we mask those feelings by telling ourselves that they must be lucky, cheating, or not very happy anyway. It is difficult to admit we are feeling envious because it carries with it an admission that we see ourselves as less than someone else. The emotion has been cast in such a negative light that it is disowned with great fervour if ever identified in another and, worse yet, never identified within ourselves. I get envious of people all the time and it feels good to admit that because truth gives me power. I know exactly what I am feeling, why and how I can use it to level up.

Types of Envy

All forms of envy can be painful but it cannot be totally avoided, and to pretend it does not exist does more harm than good. Comparing ourselves to others helps us to make sense of the world and as social beings it serves as affirmation that we are doing the human thing right. When you walk into a room and notice that everyone is formally dressed and you are in a tank top, it communicates to you that you got the dress code wrong and might need to go throw on a blazer. But on a more meaningful level it is that comparison that tells a baby that it must eventually come off its knees and begin to walk because that is how those who look like me move around.

Constructive comparison becomes envy when we use other people's progress or achievements as measures of our own self-worth and as markers for how fast or slow we should be moving.

Benign Envy: This is the 'level-up' form of envy. You observe your coworker get the employee of the year award and you step your game up so you can be in contention next year. Had you not seen someone receive the award you might not have desired it, but their achievement triggers a desire in you. You now have something to motivate you into action and achievement.

Malicious Envy: This is the 'level-down' form of envy and causes you to assess whether your coworker deserves the award and begin to undermine and perhaps sabotage their future endeavours. You don't want the award but you certainly don't want to see them with it.

ture endeavours. You don't want the award but you certainly don't want to see them with it. This negative form of envy leads to what the Germans call **schadenfreude,** where we begin to derive positive feelings at the sight of someone once celebrated being cut down.

Be careful how you allow envy to motivate you. If you are caught in the downward schadenfreude experience you are at the most dangerous point. Ask yourself why you want to see or celebrate another's failure. How does that improve your life conditions? What does that say about your personality? If another's failure gives you joy what, then, is the real quality of your joy? When you find yourself rejoicing in someone's loss it is almost certainly proof that you are envious.

The other interesting observation is that we feel this malicious and malignant envy based on our proximity to the person in question. No one feels malicious envy towards Oprah. We feel the motivational kind. She is a black billionaire, I want to be a black billionaire too. Oprah is an anomaly in our eyes because we don't know her or anyone else like her. She is a role model. It is an entirely different case when you think about an old college roommate who is now raking in millions. Their proximity to us somewhat tells us that we are the same and therefore should have access to the same luxuries. How come they have and we lack? Life is unfair and they are not more deserving than we are. Proximity makes all the difference. That explains why your cousin might support Rihanna's make-up collection but will never buy one of your handmade bags. It's less threatening to support and model those we feel are different and special than those we believe to be on our level.

Once you begin to understand the relationship between that FOMO which keeps you looking, checking, measuring, and comparing you will see the dangerous door it opens to social envy. The other dimension of this FOMO experience is the fact that we might well be alone. Loneliness and the anxiety that accompanies carry emotional and physical burdens that are difficult to contextualise. People need people, and there is no substitute for real human contact. Living alone, being without friends, lacking an intimate partner to pair-bond with can all act as stimuli for a lonely, depressive state. Even something as simple as touch has the power to extend our lives.

The fear of being alone can actually cause us to isolate ourselves in anticipation of a life without love and support. It can also lead to, and keep us in, unhealthy relationships because we would rather have bad company than none at all.

In 1990, after the fall of Communism, the world got a glimpse of how the deprivation of human contact, affection, and touch coupled with physical and sexual abuse impacted the growth and development of orphans in Romania. These children had be abandoned, displaced by war and separated from their families as toddlers. What researchers found was that they suffered from stunted growth (some 20-year olds looking no older than six or seven years); psychological trauma, insecure attachment to foster families and death.

In 1944 a United States based experiment found that even when babies were given food, health check-ups, regular baths, and a safe environment, they would still die if their caregivers did not touch them or communicate with them. People **need** people. Loneliness and isolation are directly connected to our mortality, unlike any other major fear. To properly kill the fear it is important to identify its source(see Chapter 3). If you are unable to identify the source on your own you will need to seek help from a trained professional. The next step is to identify how that fear is driving your behaviour. It may be carrying you to one of two extremes. Either you have serious discomfort being alone and compensate by keeping the TV on when you're home so it feels like you have company, or you cultivate unhealthy relationships to keep your space full of people.

Some choose to become serial monogamists to avoid being without a partner or serial conversationalists spending hours on the phone in meaningless conversations just to avoid silence. Either way the problem is the same - a fear of loneliness.

For those of us capable of doing our own self-assessment we will find that we are afraid of being alone because we have handed over the care of ourselves to someone else. Our emotional and physical well-being has become tied to others in a way that is unhealthy. We fear exiting the abusive marriage or stagnant friendship because we fear not being able to find someone else to meet the needs we have. Developing trust in your ability to care for you is the first step to liberating your spirit from the unhealthy need to be 'peopled'. That belief that no matter how bad things are it is better than being alone must be abandoned. In fact, it is better to be alone than to be abused and mistreated if you master the gifts of your solitude.

This is a lesson I am still learning. I grew up hating silence and solitude. I was cultured to think it was some form of punishment, not having any one to talk to or being without some kind of noise or distraction. I discovered this in my early 20s when I was living on my own and going through the most painful break-up you could imagine. What made it so painful was that I couldn't hate the person I was being separated from. As they dealt with their own fear of commitment I had to deal with my fear of loneliness and that was overwhelming. I couldn't get angry at him for cheating because he didn't. I couldn't get angry at him for being abusive because he wasn't. I couldn't get angry at him for being dishonest because he hadn't been. It is so much easier to comfort yourself through pain when you can blame and hate someone else for your misery. When you have to take full responsibility there is a special type of courage that you feel need to reprimand and repair yourself.

He was just not ready to commit and I took that as the ultimate form of rejection. I got caught reflecting on what this loss would cost me and how lonely I would be without him and how impossible it would be to find someone who made me as happy as he did. I was happy because of him, focused because of him, excited about the future because of him. Cropping him out of the picture meant I had to find all those things on my own and I really didn't want to. But I realised I had to. If I was to add value to any relationship I had to be whole on my own.

I started to get comfortable in my solitude. I embraced not having anyone to tell me goodnight in hushed tones. I accepted that the only "You're beautiful" I would hear would come from me looking in the mirror and saying it to myself. I had to start getting my Brazilian waxes done for me because no one would be seeing them for a while. I had to listen to my favourite love songs and see me loving me. I had to bring myself to ME. It was a long walk to get to a place of personal happiness and confidence but here I am. And even in this brand new relationship where I don't have to be alone, I deliberately carve out time to be by myself, with my thoughts, pain and anxieties.

HOW TO FIRE

To Kill FOMO: Own Your Envy

You must deliberately change the station from "Them TV" to "Me TV". Your frequency must be tuned to you. You can only get distracted or exhausted based on what you are focusing on. If you take the focus away from others and put it on yourself, the negative emotions tend to diminish. But you must own your envy. Admit what you feel and take the time to interrogate it. Do you actually want the thing that you're envious about? Probably not. Would you be willing to work as hard as they have worked to achieve that? Probably not.

Yes, they have what you don't have. Yes, they go where you've never been. Yes, they know what you don't know and have all the degrees to prove it. Yes, they look, sound, and smell flawless. And that is all ok. Don't go to war with your precious self. Forgive yourself for not knowing, seeing and being…yet. Life isn't running out on you and what is for sure is that you have a host of blessings to be enamoured and distracted by if you would only pay attention to YOU. Having all doesn't make you happy. The joy comes from having what matters to you.

Here's where you start - Abundance. There is no less success left over because someone out there is massively successful. All of basketball's glory didn't leave the NBA with Michael Jordon. Every season new players emerge making hundreds of millions of dollars. The success didn't run out.

All the beautiful homes didn't stop being built because your high school rival bought his. There is more. There is always more left. More love, more success, more happiness for wealth, more promotions. Tackle that fear of missing out with a blow to the kneecaps. There is always more. When we switch stations and depart from the scarcity perspective; that there isn't enough or it will run out before we get them, it brings us more peace. We don't feel hastened to act, prove, go, or say. We become confident in our skills and look to align those with our purpose. Not to compete with someone else but to fulfil our divine and unique destinies. That's all your business. Only you can manage it and absolutely no one can take it from you. See life from a position of abundance.

My gratitude journal helps me to check in daily on my blessings. It is a tool that helps to mute the noise of all that is missing and amplify the sweet sounds of my daily, perpetual blessings.

Another useful tool to mute the noise is to turn off the notifications - literally. There are several apps that you can add to your phone that will also prevent you from using social media apps outside of a scheduled time. Try Offtime, Moment, Breakfree, or App Detox if you find yourself over-connecting, over-watching, or over-sharing. Reduce the time spent watching how others live and recommit to the process of designing and pursuing the life you want. Make time for real human connection and conversation instead of perpetually observing the sanitised versions of people's lives and comparing it to your normal. Get real again. Don't build your life around technology, let technology serve you. If Facebook connects you to a high school friend use the messenger app instead of the comment bar and invite them to drinks so you can catch up. That in person conversation does more for your well-being and that relationship than any number of heart eyes under their wedding anniversary photo.

Let's get real again.

> *We all come into the world with insecurities that can easily be amplified because of how much of others and their success we are now able to see.*

To Kill Loneliness: Find YOU

No one can walk into your life and cure you. The healing of your deepest scars is your responsibility. Stop waiting for someone to find you and make you whole and start pulling yourself together a day at a time. Some of us will need medication to do it, others of us won't. But what we will all need is to get comfortable enough with ourselves to not fear the days when we are all that we have.

Purposeful breathing, meditation, reading, and journaling are some ways to get comfortable with your feelings, your body, and your blessings. In these moments when you are alone you begin to prepare for a life of balance in place of co-dependency. You also come to a place of increased mindfulness as you generate greater awareness of what you need to be happy instead of what you need to do to make someone else happy. Attack that feeling of empty with a feeling of enough.

Finding you means listening and learning what you need to fill your tank before you go searching for passengers. Despite how many people you take along for the ride, if you don't have the fuel to sustain the ride you won't finish the journey. Even worse, you run the risk of ruining the lives of others because no matter how great your backseat driver is, if you're not ready to be behind the wheel you will very likely wreck the car and hurt those travelling with you.

Find you.
Friend you.
Fuel you.

And in the end...

Once you have killed fear you will begin to stand out. You will look different to those who knew you before. This new-found boldness will make some people cautious or even envious of who you have become. Do not be surprised if you can't fit into the small spaces that used to be home.

Henry David Thoreau said, "envy is the tax which all distinction must pay". While we romanticise what it must feel like to have all eyes on us and everyone green with envy for what we have, it is no place of glory. Those who have spent even a few moments being envied because of their success will tell you how distrusting and uncomfortable it makes them of and around others. Some perhaps believe that it is wise to stay in the shadows unseen and unheard to avoid becoming the victim of that gutter-green emotion.

Standing out in a crowd has its benefits, but for many of us those rare moments of being dragged back down to 'size', ridiculed and ostracised are enough to keep us from ever taking a risk and using our voices again. This fear is not one that we conjure up. It is one that society carefully crafts and goes to lengths to nourish. It is very real and for those of us who choose to stand out, it is very painful.

None of us wants to be put under a microscope and have our every move examined and judged but that is a consequence of distinction. None of us wants to be on the receiving end of those "oh my God, she just won't shut up" stares. Unfortunately, that is all part of the journey to excellence. People won't like that you are bold enough to do more than you are told and be more than they gave you permission to be. It flies in the face of their own influence and the power they believe they have over your life. Get ready for the blowback because you have fired a shot and cracked the glass case that they have put you in. They won't see how hard you worked to kill your fears but that's quite fine. The journey is yours and the life you are fighting to save is your own. Wish them well on their journey and continue on with yours.

Excellence makes people uncomfortable.

To avoid the victimisation, the unkind comments and the awkward stares, you will be tempted to sit down. But that fear you feel is proof of the power of the influence you can have. It can be scary, but this is my favourite fear to kill. I actually have fun doing it. I embrace the fact that I will be ridiculed and look silly to some. I accept that nothing extraordinary comes from averages, but from outliers. I get excited at the thought that none have gone before and I may be in for some kind of unique achievement. I kill fear and I stand out.

For women this takes profound effort because standing out is seen as a masculine trait. The polite and feminine thing to do is smile and nod; agree and acquiesce. It is considered uncharacteristic to stand out on your own platform instead of waiting to be introduced by a person of influence. You can tell that it is unexpected when you compare the feedback, whether positive or negative, to what might be said if a man made a similar move.

When he stands out he is described as brave, a risk taker.

Kill Fear

When she stands out it is seen as novel (because it is hardly ever done), but her celebration comes with a caution: Be careful that you don't become too much. The idea of being too much asks us to consider the view of others and tread lightly lest they come to see us as overbearing.

As a child, an over achieving and well awarded student would be given the distinguishing label "nuff", an abridged version of the word "enough", which is meant to mock one's excellence. It is meant to say that you have literally done quite enough and should stop. In other words, you are too much. Those slights communicated to me as a child that being too much was a bad thing, that there was some invisible line of achievement beyond which one should not go lest you draw the ire and dislike of those around you. This fear is intimately linked to the fear of people's opinions. So as not to be disliked or badmouthed we dial down our excellence and blend right in. If they can't see us they can't criticise us, right?

If you answered yes I hope you can feel your influence and achievement slipping through your fingers.

Standing with the herd meets a deep psychological need to feel connected. Swimming against the tide exposes us to the likelihood of being ostracised and having to stand alone with no support from the team. It is a fear embedded in our genetics as humans; a well-aged fear some 200,000 years old. You are not crazy to feel immobilised by the thought of standing out because it feels like you're putting your life on the line.

This fear and its power to dissolve human dignity and identity is the basis on which our justice system is founded.

Criminals are sent to prison on the basis that the ostracism teaches them a psychological lesson. A more profound punishment is being sent to solitary confinement, again because of its psychological power to distort the way we view ourselves and the world. Loneliness or the threat of it is crippling.

But these are the extremes. We know that standing out at work won't lead to us being sent to the hole, but just the thought that we may use the favour of others seems to have a similar effect. But that is just our brain's natural hyperbolic interpretation of what would actually happen. Yes you will draw the ugly stares and a few unkind remarks but showing your distinct talent and abilities are hardly grounds to get you kicked out of your job. In this half of the century it might all be your one-way ticket to a promotion.

The world has changed. Blending into the herd is no longer the premise for being celebrated. You hear it all the time. New businesses are looking for disruptors, people willing to raise the bar and push the envelope. While the sentiments in the room remain, the one in charge might just be looking for someone willing to stand out. Conformists are fast losing their appeal. They make everyone comfortable but they inspire no one and progress needs inspiration.

Remember the world is changed by outliers.

Do not conform. Do not dial it down. Don't turn down the shine for fear of who it will blind. You are a masterpiece and you have every right to be on that pedestal. Just like anyone else willing to earn excellence.

Whatever they said made you unqualified or unworthy - gender, age, sexuality, social status - was all fabricated fluff. The truth is, you make them uncomfortable, but your divine essence was placed here to help them grow beyond their illusions and discomfort. You may very well be the catalyst they need, so be YOU. Be your EXCELLENT you!

It hardly matters what is "expected" in a world where mediocrity is celebrated and is excellence viciously scrutinised. You'll want to fit in, to be regular and normal and liked and all the boring things that under-performers are always talking about. Tell them you're not interested and refuse to be impressed by anything less than excellence. Then you start living like you mean it!

It is your right and duty to become all you can be. One of my favourite verses from the Bible also happens to be the motto for my alma mater and it affirms the God-given instruction that we are meant to illuminate this earth.

In the same way, let your light shine before others, so that they may see your good works and give glory to your Father who is in heaven. ~ Matthew 5:16

Own your birthright

Always choose your highest calling. Do not be held captive by:

- Ideas on who you SHOULD be
- Anxiety about what you COULD do
- Shame about what you HAVE DONE.

Set yourself free with the knowledge of who you WILL BE when you tap into your innate strength, your earth-shattering energy...

when you choose your highest calling.

Have you ever wondered why those who stand out get further ahead? It is because they get noticed. People pay attention and because the world can't pay attention to everyone, the glamour and fame work better when we have just a controlled set of "Incredibles". But that premise is proving itself to be false. We seem to always make room for a new movie star or pop star or sporting giant. There is always room for more stars once they earn their place in the sky.

Get noticed for the right reasons and watch how the initial disdain and disgust will morph into admiration. But if you stand in the crowd, who sees or hears you? How will they know what you have to offer? How will you get the right eyes on your skills and unique energy? You have to choose to surge ahead and stand out.

Everyone has the potential to be extraordinary. The good news is, so few people even bother to try. That puts the odds in your favour. Work your odds.

When you live below your potential, who do you think suffers the greatest loss? The world already has enough mediocre minds coming up with mediocre solutions to get mediocre results. How about you introduce some excellence in your environment today?

So, Gladiator:

Enter the arena. Win the war between your ears. Let your potential lead you. Every day, live with courage. Every day, **KILL FEAR!**

References

Binazir, A. (2011, June 16). Are you a miracle? On the probability of your being born.
Retrieved from https://www.huffingtonpost.com/dr-ali-binazir/probability-being-born_b_877853.html

Brown, B. (2017). Braving the wilderness. The quest for true belonging and the courage to stand
alone. New York: Random House.

Greater Good Science Centre. (2015). Self-compassion break. Retrieved from https://ggia.berkeley. edu/practice/self_compassion_break

Marche, S. (2012, May). Is Facebook making us lonely?. The Atlantic. Retrieved from https://www.theatlantic.com/magazine/archive/2012/05/is-facebook-making-us-lonely/308930/

Primack, B. A., Shensa, A., Sidani, J. E., Whaite, E. O., Lin, L. Y., Rosen, D., Colditz, J. B., Radovic,
A., & Miller, E. (2017). Social media use and perceived social isolation among young adults in the U.S. American Journal of Preventative Medicine, 53(1). 1-8. doi.org/10.1016/j.amepre.2017.01.010

Przybylski, A. K., Murayama, K., DeHaan, C. R., & Gladwell, V. (2013). Motivational, emotional, and behavioral correlates of fear of missing out. Computers in Human Behavior. 29 (4), 1841- 1848. doi.org/10.1016/j.chb.2013.02.014

Shakespeare, W. (1873). Measure for measure London: Longman's, Green and Co. [TED]. (2015, February 16). How to practice emotional first aid | Guy Winch.[Video File]. Retrieved
from https://www.youtube.com/watch?v=F2hc2FLOdhI

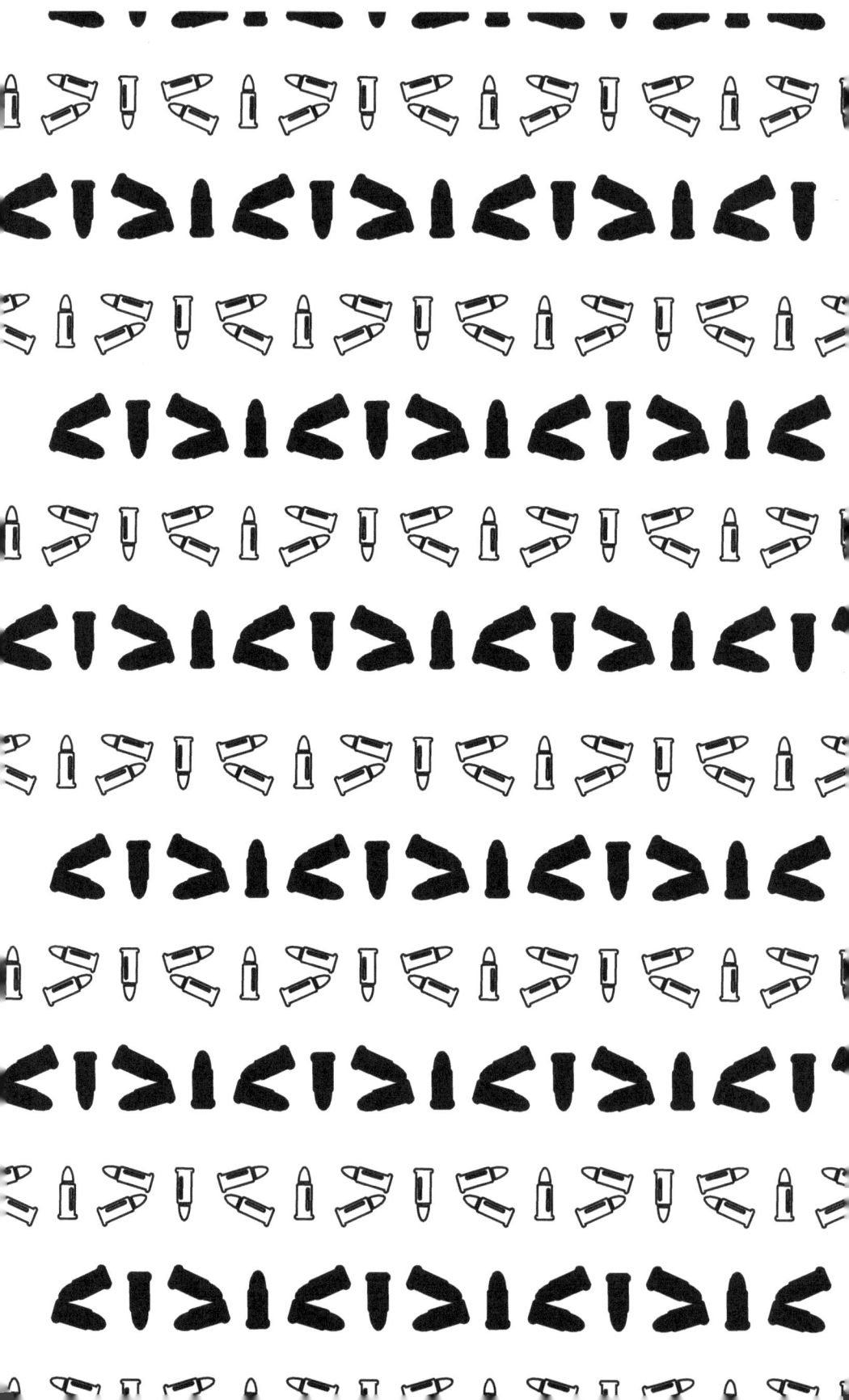

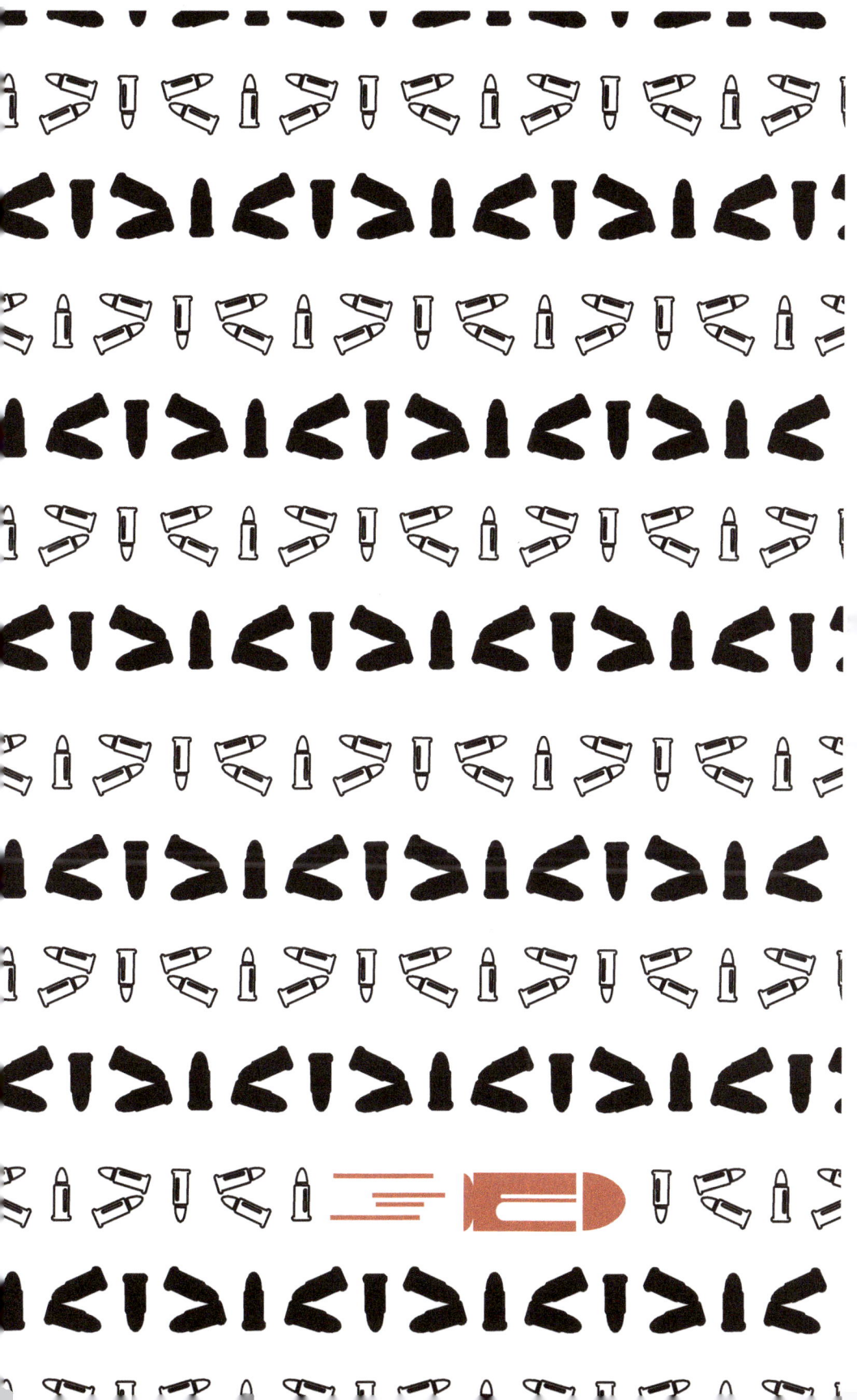

www.ingramcontent.com/pod-product-compliance
Lightning Source LLC
Chambersburg PA
CBHW062111290426
44110CB00023B/2780